Great Ideas

Listening and speaking activities
for students of American English

Student's Book

Leo Jones

Victoria Kimbrough

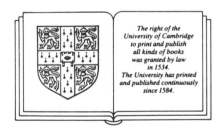

The right of the
University of Cambridge
to print and publish
all kinds of books
was granted by law
in 1534.
The University has printed
and published continuously
since 1584.

Cambridge University Press

Cambridge
New York   Port Chester
Melbourne   Sydney

Published by the Press Syndicate of the University of Cambridge
The Pitt Building, Trumpington Street, Cambridge CB2 1RP
32 East 57th Street, New York, NY 10022, USA
10 Stamford Road, Oakleigh, Melbourne 3166, Australia

© Cambridge University Press 1987

First published 1987
Fourth printing 1989

Printed in the United States of America

Library of Congress Cataloging-in-Publication Data
Jones, Leo, 1943–

Great ideas.

1. English language – Text-books for foreign
speakers.   2. English language – Spoken English –
United States.   3. Listening.   I. Kimbrough,
Victoria, 1943 –   .   II. Title.
PE1128.J633   1987   428.3′4   86-26824
ISBN 0 521 31242 6 (student's book)
ISBN 0 521 31243 4 (teacher's manual)
ISBN 0 521 32052 6 (cassette)

Contents

Introduction

To the student

This book is about ideas: about listening to and understanding other people's ideas, communicating your own ideas, and above all, exchanging ideas with your fellow students. There is a wide variety of activities in this book – there are problems to solve, discussions to participate in, roles to play, and tasks to complete – but they all have one thing in common: They will give you plenty to talk about.

Pairs and groups   Most of the activities will involve you in talking to partners in small groups or in pairs. There are several reasons why this is valuable: (1) You don't have to worry about mistakes.   (2) Everyone has time to communicate their own ideas.   (3) Each activity can become a real conversation – not just a piece of "language practice."

What about mistakes?   You can't learn how to speak a foreign language without making mistakes. The question is: How much do they matter? Is it more important to speak 100% accurately or to learn to communicate effectively? If you're afraid to express an idea because you may make a mistake, then you won't make any progress. Mistakes can tell you what you will need to learn. So don't be afraid of mistakes. Your partners and your teacher will correct the ones that seem to prevent you from communicating – but don't expect every mistake you make to be corrected.

Listening exercises 🔲   The exercises recorded on the Cassette are linked to realistic "tasks" – charts for you to fill in, diagrams to draw, notes to make, and so on. In real life we listen to find out about other people's ideas and new information. And when we have understood all this, we relate it to our own experience and use it in our own conversations. After each listening exercise you'll have a chance to discuss what you found out.

Communication activities   The 88 communication activities at the back of the book give different information to each partner in a group. There is an "information gap" between you: Your purpose is to find out what your partners know and to tell them what you know. Related communication activities are all on separate pages so that you can't read each other's information. The instructions in each unit tell you which activity to turn to at the back of the book.

The activities in *Great Ideas* will help you to enjoy using English, but make sure that you continue widening your vocabulary and improving your grammatical accuracy. Keep on asking questions!

To the teacher

There is a separate Teacher's Manual for *Great Ideas* containing detailed teaching notes, warm-up and additional activities, suggested answers to exercises, and tape-scripts corresponding to the listening exercises recorded on the Cassette.

1 You and me

LISTENING ACTIVITY: WHAT ARE YOUR AMBITIONS? 🔊

1. You are going to hear four people answer questions on a radio program. As you listen to the tape, complete the following chart. Listen to the recording as many times as necessary to get all the answers.

	1st speaker: (David George)	2nd speaker: (Suzanne Brown)	3rd speaker: (Adolfo Vasquez)	4th speaker: (Linda Montgomery)
1. What is the speaker's job?				
2. What does he or she do for fun?				
3. What exciting thing has happened recently?				
4. Who does the speaker admire most?				
5. What does the speaker want to be doing in 5 years?				

2. Compare your notes with a partner. Discuss which of the speakers you think you would get along with best.

1.2 **COMMUNICATION ACTIVITY: RADIO SURVEY**

Now it's your turn to participate. You are going to take part in a survey by a radio station. Work in pairs. One of you should look at communication activity 4. The other should turn to activity 20. The communication activities are at the back of the book.

When you have finished, discuss with your partner which questions and which answers were the most interesting.

Look at the young woman in this photograph.
Work in pairs.
What kind of person do you think she is?
How would you describe her mood?

Here are some more pictures of the same young woman in different moods.
Take turns describing the photographs. Get your partner to guess which picture
    you're describing. (Don't start with the first picture.)
Here are some adjectives you can use: embarrassed, nervous, worried, puzzled,
    excited, curious, confused, pensive, wistful, exasperated.
You can also say:
She looks like *she's daydreaming*.

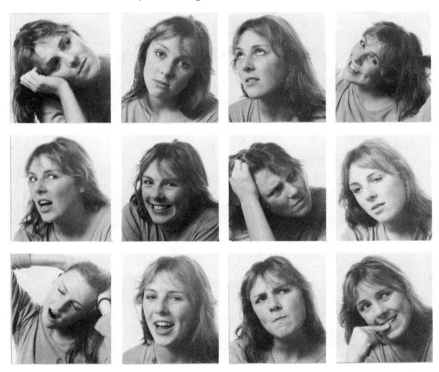

Work in pairs. Discuss these questions:
a) What mood are you in now?
b) Which pictures show the moods you feel the most often?
c) Do you have rapid changes of mood?
d) Do you show your feelings in your expressions or in the way you speak?
    Or do you tend to hide your feelings?

Look at the adjectives below. Decide with a partner which of them you can use to describe each of the other people in your class – and yourselves, too. Try to find at least three for each person in the class. Use a dictionary to find the meanings of the words you don't know.

artistic	efficient	good-natured	loyal	rational
capable	energetic	happy	open-minded	self-confident
careful	enthusiastic	hardworking	optimistic	sensible
cheerful	flexible	helpful	organized	sensitive
considerate	frank	humorous	outgoing	spontaneous
creative	friendly	imaginative	patient	thoughtful
dependable	generous	intelligent	perceptive	unselfish
diplomatic	gentle	interesting	polite	versatile
easygoing	good-humored	kind	practical	witty

1.5   WHAT KIND OF PERSON ARE YOU?

Take the following personality quiz.

Do you see yourself as others see you?
by DR. CHARLES VINE

It is no good looking into a mirror if you wish to see the *real* you. The real test is to see yourself as others see you, and the following test can let you do just that . . .
     Circle your answers to the questions below.

1. When do you feel your best?
  (a) In the morning.
  (b) During the afternoon and early evening.
  (c) Late at night.

2. Do you usually walk
  (a) fairly fast, with long steps?
  (b) fairly fast, but with short, quick steps?
  (c) less fast, head up, looking the world in the face?
  (d) less fast, head down?
  (e) very slowly?

3. When talking to people, do you
  (a) stand with your arms folded?
  (b) have your hands clasped?
  (c) have one or both hands on your hips?
  (d) touch or push the person to whom you are talking?
  (e) play with your ear, touch your chin, or smooth your hair?

"Little Susie Miller all grown up."

Drawing by Frascino; © 1978 The New Yorker Magazine, Inc.

4. When relaxing, do you sit with
   (a) your knees bent and your legs neatly side by side?
   (b) your legs crossed?
   (c) your legs stretched out or straight?
   (d) with one leg curled under you?
5. When something really amuses you, how do you react? Do you give
   (a) a big, appreciative laugh?
   (b) a laugh, but not a loud one?
   (c) a quiet chuckle?
   (d) a big smile?
   (e) a slow smile?
6. When you go to a party or social gathering, do you
   (a) make a loud entrance so everyone notices you?
   (b) make a quieter entrance, looking around quickly for someone you know?
   (c) make the quietest possible entrance and try to stay unnoticed?
7. You are working hard, concentrating hard. You're interrupted. Do you
   (a) welcome the break?
   (b) feel extremely irritated?
   (c) vary between these two extremes?

8. Which of the following colors do you like most?
   (a) Red or orange.
   (b) Black.
   (c) Yellow or light blue.
   (d) Green.
   (e) Dark blue or purple.
   (f) White.
   (g) Brown, gray, or violet.
9. When you are in bed at night, in those last few moments before going to sleep, do you lie
   (a) stretched out on your back?
   (b) stretched out face down on your stomach?
   (c) on your side, slightly curled?
   (d) with your head on one arm?
   (e) with your head under the covers?
10. Do you often dream that you are
    (a) falling?
    (b) fighting or struggling?
    (c) searching for someone or something?
    (d) flying or floating?
    (e) Or do you usually have a dreamless sleep?
    (f) Or do you have pleasant dreams?

1.6   COMMUNICATION ACTIVITY: SCORING YOUR QUIZ

How well do you know yourself? Turn to activity 84 for instructions on how to interpret the personality quiz.

Afterward, work in pairs. Talk to your partner about the results of the quiz, and discuss these questions.

— What did you find out about your personality?
— Do you agree with the interpretation of the quiz?
— Can questions like these really show someone's personality?

Useful expressions

I think/don't think that I . . .   *I didn't know that you . . .*
Do you think that I . . . ?   *I always thought that you . . .*
I'm not really sure whether . . .   *Do you really . . . ?*
I never thought that I . . .   *I was surprised to find . . .*

Work with a partner and try to solve the following problems. Do each activity with a different partner and be sure you work out the answer *together* – not on your own.

1. Look at this photo and decide what's going on. Make up a story to show what happened before and after it was taken. Tell your story to another pair.

2. Put the sentences in the right order for the following stories.

   a) When I returned to the dormitory, I said proudly, "I gave blood."
   "Wow," said my roommate.
   I finally got up enough courage to give blood at the blood-donor center.
   "You'll do anything to lose weight!"

   b) "Yes, " he replied, "but you were going the wrong way!"
   He scolded me for doing such a "crazy thing."
   The leader of my church was a little shocked when he heard that I had just made my first parachute jump with a sky-divers club.
   "But," I said, "I was so close to heaven up there."

   c) While visiting my brother, I borrowed $50 from him.
   He called me up and told me how much he enjoyed my letters, regardless of the money: I had never written regularly before.
   In my mail box the next week I found an envelope from my brother.
   After my return home, I wrote him a short letter every few weeks, enclosing a five-dollar check in each one.
   Inside was another $50.
   Finally I sent off a letter and the last five-dollar check.

Anecdotes reprinted by permission from *Reader's Digest*. (a) Contributed by Norma Safford, (b) contributed by Pam Nelson, and (c) contributed by Suzanne Attebery.

2 Stranger than fiction

2.1 **LISTENING ACTIVITY: 1900** 🔲

Coincidences* are very hard to explain logically. Listen to this conversation about two Italians named Vittorio, and write down all the coincidences you hear.

1	5
2	6
3	7
4	8

Work in pairs and compare your lists. Discuss the coincidences.
Were they all just chance? If not, how do you explain them? Find out what your partner thinks.

* *Coincidence*: When events happen at the same time by accident but seem to have some connection.

2.2 **COMMUNICATION ACTIVITY: 100 YEARS' DIFFERENCE**

Work in pairs. These pictures represent two people who lived 100 years apart. Who do you think they are? What do you know about them?
When you have decided, or if you can't decide at all, one of you should look at activity 11, and the other at activity 41.

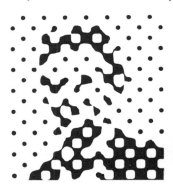 

Useful expressions

I think that's . . . *I recognize . . . He was . . .*
That looks like it might be . . . *I don't know much about . . .*
Wasn't he . . . ? *I have no idea who/what . . .*
Weren't they both . . . ? *He looks like/resembles . . .*

Read the following true story. Then work with a partner and list all the coincidences you can find.

James Springer of Dayton, Ohio, and James Lewis of Lima, Ohio, are identical twins who met for the first time at the age of 39. They were each adopted by different couples, who named them both James. Each was told that his brother had died at birth. Springer has been married twice. His first wife's name was Linda, and his second wife's name is Betty. Lewis has been married three times. His first wife was named Linda and his second wife was named Betty. One named his son James Allan, the other James Alan. Springer has a dog named Toy, and Lewis had a dog named Toy when he was a child. Each has the same hobbies, goes to the same vacation resort in Florida, drinks the same brand of beer, smokes the same kind of cigarettes, liked the same subject – math – in high school, and has had law-enforcement training. They are the same height and weight, and both have high blood pressure.

Probably no one in your class is your long-lost twin. But you may have more in common with your classmates than you think! Go around the class and talk to as many people as you can. Find out if anyone:

was born on the same day as you;

is the same age as you;

likes the same sports, subjects in school, and entertainment as you;

has the same astrological sign and the same kind of personality as you;

has the same number of brothers and sisters;

has the same habits as you.

Useful expressions

What day were you born?
Oh, I am/do/did/was too!
I'm not/I don't/I didn't/I wasn't either!
Do you like . . . ?
I like . . . . What about you?

What did you like to do when you
*   were a child?*
I used to . . .
Me too!
Not me.

Jeane Dixon, a famous psychic, can apparently read people's minds and foresee the future.
– Once she begged her husband not to take a plane. At the last minute he took the train. The plane crashed.
– One night she walked into a party and told the people there exactly what they had been doing before she arrived.
– Another time she looked at the picture of a girl she had never seen before and got up and started walking just like the girl. The girl's father was amazed – his daughter had a medical problem and could not walk normally.

Work in small groups or pairs and discuss these questions.
a) Do you believe in ESP (extrasensory perception)? Can some people read minds or foresee the future?
b) Have you ever heard of incidents like the ones above? Tell your partner about them.
c) Have you ever foreseen an event or had a feeling that something was going to happen? Do you know anyone who has?

Work with a partner and write out as many superstitions as you can think of. For example:

It's bad luck to walk under a ladder.
If a black cat walks in front of you, you'll have bad luck.

_____

_____

_____

_____

_____

_____

Work in small groups and discuss the following questions.
a) Have any of the above things ever happened to you? Did you have good or bad luck afterward?
b) Where do you think superstitions come from?
c) Do you believe that your future is already determined or do you think you make your own future?
d) Do you think we can create our own good luck or bad luck by what we believe? Or are some people just naturally lucky or unlucky?

Work in pairs. One of you should look at activity 14 and the other at activity 25. When you finish, tell the class why you think your partner is or isn't superstitious.

2.7   IS IT ALL IN THE MIND?

Many things happen in the world that we cannot explain. Work in small groups and discuss the following mysterious phenomena. What are *your* answers to the questions?

GHOSTS: Many people say that they have seen or heard ghosts. Do you think
they exist?
THE BERMUDA TRIANGLE: Why have over 100 ships and planes disappeared in
this area, with the loss of 1,000 lives?
UFOs: Are unidentified flying objects (UFOs) spaceships from another planet?
CLAIRVOYANCE: Can some people see objects hidden behind a wall, or see objects
that are miles away?
ASTROLOGY: Do the stars and planets influence personality and behavior?
REINCARNATION: When people die, do they return to earth as someone or
something else?
ESP (extrasensory perception): Can some people read other people's minds and know
what is going to happen in the future?
FATE: Do human beings control their own future or is it already determined?
TELEPATHY: Can some people read minds and know what other people are
thinking?
PREDICTING THE FUTURE: Can some people see the future by looking into a
crystal ball, or reading someone's palm, or using cards?

Can you think of other mysterious happenings in the world that cannot be explained?
What do you think about them?

Work in pairs. Make up stories
to explain these pictures.
Imagine you were one of the
people in the picture. Decide
what happened before and
after each picture was taken.

3   Can I help you?

Discuss the picture in pairs or small groups.
a) What do you think of clothes like these?
b) Would you ever wear them? If so, where?
c) Do you like to wear very stylish clothes or clothes that are more classic?
d) Do you prefer to wear informal or formal clothes?
e) What kind of informal clothes do you like?

Useful expressions

That's (not) my style.
I like to wear ...
I like clothes that are ...
I'd rather buy ... than ...
I almost never buy ...

I can't stand ...
I don't think I'd ever ...
I (don't) think clothes are really
   important because ...

Work with a partner and imagine you are looking for the following things. What kind of store would you need to go to?

shoelaces	an electric shaver
a watch	a pair of left-handed scissors
airmail envelopes	a screwdriver
a second-hand guitar	a gold toothpick
a pair of hand-made cowboy boots	a diamond ring
a set of wine glasses	a box of chocolate-covered cherries

If you need some help thinking of stores, turn to communication activity 83.
Next the class will be divided into two groups: A and B. Group B will be the store-owners and Group A will be their customers. Group A should turn to communication activity 54 and Group B to activity 12.

3.3   LISTENING ACTIVITY: A SHOPPING SPREE

You are going to hear a husband and wife tell each other what they bought. Fill in the missing information in the chart below.

Name of the store	What did the man/woman buy there?	Who bought it?
Tip-Top		
The Gap		
Macy's		
McDonald's		

3.4   COMMUNICATION ACTIVITY: SPENDING MONEY

Work in pairs and get your partner's opinion about shopping. One of you should look at communication activity 75, and the other at activity 42. When you have finished, report your findings to the class.

Work with a partner. Imagine that one of you is going to a country in Asia and the other to the United States or Canada. Decide which country you are going to and tell your partner. Then, think of some things you would like from your partner's country, and ask him or her to bring them back for you. Don't worry about trying to save money — just choose things that are "typical" or things that perhaps you can't get in your country.

When you finish, decide with your partner what *three* things a foreign visitor to *your* country should take home.

food ?
Clothes ?
Electronic Equipment ?
(NOT stereo - too heavy!)
Records ?
Books ?
Antiques ?
Household Goods ?
Tourist Souvenirs?

Useful expressions

Do you think you would have room to bring me . . . ?
Would you have time to look for . . . ?

I'd really like to have . . .
Can you get . . . in . . . ?
I know it's crazy, but I'd love . . .

Imagine that you just won a small prize in a contest. You want to use the money to buy a small, very inexpensive present for everyone in your class. Work in pairs or small groups and decide what your group would buy each person. Be sure you choose something the person would like or might need. Don't forget your teacher!
When you are ready, tell your classmates what your group is going to give them.

Useful expressions

He likes (to) . . . , so we could give him . . .
I think she'd like . . . , because . . .
What do you think . . . would like?
How much does . . . cost?

I don't think he'd like . . . , because . . .
I think she'd like . . . better.
We can't get him that, because . . .
We're giving her . . . , because . . .

Look around the room and pick out five items your classmates have or are wearing that you admire. Write down the items to help you remember. Look at the different ways to compliment people below, and then go and compliment your classmates.

You can start with:
That's a beautiful (pretty, nice, fantastic, great) . . .
Those are really nice (pretty, good-looking, great) . . .
I really like your . . .

You can continue with:
Is it (are they) new?
Where did you get it (them)?
I like the color (style, material).
You look good in (color).

The most common answer to a compliment is, "Thank you." You could also say, "I'm glad you like it" or "I got it at . . ."

For example:
You: That's really a beautiful blouse.
Betty: Thank you, I just got it.
You: You look good in green, and I like the high collar.
Betty: Oh, thanks.

4   What a nice day!

4.1   IN THE SNOW

Work in pairs or small groups and discuss the following questions.

What's the man doing?
How do you think he feels?
What should he have done the night before?
Have you ever had this experience or one like it?
Do you like the snow?

What kind of activities do you like to do in the snow?
If it were 0 degrees Fahrenheit (about −18 degrees Celsius), and you were cut off from the outside world with no heat or electricity, what would you do?
What is the coldest day you remember? Try to remember how it felt that day and what everyone said to each other about it.
What is the hottest day you remember? the wettest? the windiest?

Useful expressions

It's really awful to have to . . .   *It was so cold that . . .*
I don't think I would mind . . .   *I'd probably . . . if I . . .*
I like/hate the snow because . . .   *If I couldn't . . . then I'd try to . . .*

4.2   COMMUNICATION ACTIVITY: WHAT'S THE WEATHER LIKE?

You need to find out about the weather in other countries for a business trip. Work with a partner. One of you should look at activity 1 and the other at activity 50.

1. Work in pairs or small groups. Look at the map below. What do you think the weather is like in early spring (late March/early April) in these cities? For example: "I think that it's probably cold in New York in late March, maybe about 40 degrees Fahrenheit, and it probably rains a lot and is very windy."

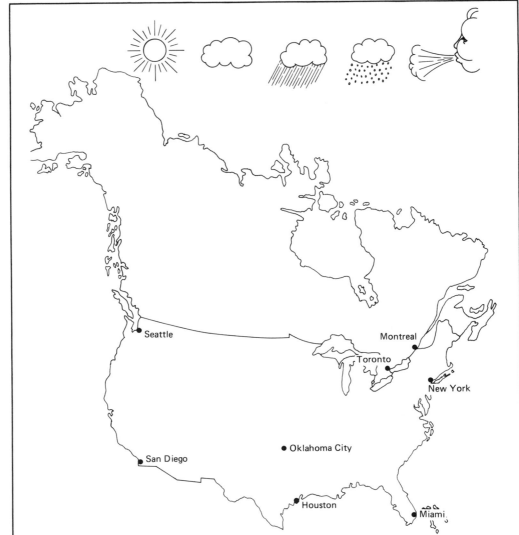

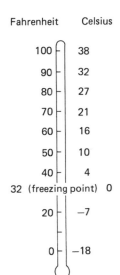

2. Listen to the weather report and write on the map the temperatures that are mentioned. Then listen again and write in the weather symbols to show what kind of weather they are having in each city.
3. Compare your work with a partner's. Did you both get the same information? Compare the weather where you are now to the weather in the places described in the report.
    Examples: It's warmer here than in Montreal.
               It's not as hot as Houston.
4. What was your weather report today?

1. Work in groups of four. What do you think the climate is like in the cities on the map? How do they compare with your own town or city? Can you guess which is the hottest and which is the coldest place? Which do you think is the driest? the wettest? What's the hottest place you've ever been? What's the coldest?

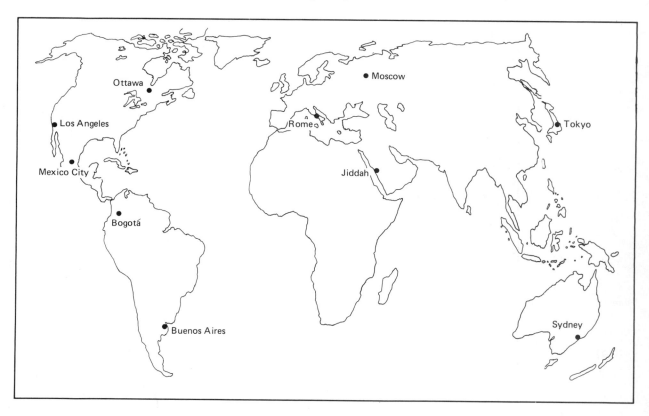

2. When you have made your guesses, two of you should look at communication activity 15, while the other two look at activity 37. You will find more details and information there.

Useful expressions

What do you think the weather's like in . . . ?
I bet . . . is the coldest place.
. . . is probably the driest place because . . .
I think I could live in . . .
I don't think I could stand . . .
It's probably really nice in . . .

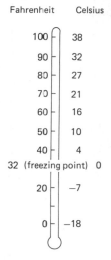

Fahrenheit	Celsius
100	38
90	32
80	27
70	21
60	16
50	10
40	4
32 (freezing point)	0
20	−7
0	−18

WHAT ELSE IS IT GOOD FOR?

Each of the things in this drawing has one obvious use. But how many *other* uses can you think of for each of them? Use your imagination and see if your group can come up with more ideas than the other groups. For example, an umbrella can be used to get something off a high shelf, to keep someone away from you, etc.

Useful expressions

You could ...
This could be used to ...
I can't think of anything else to do
  with a ...

How would you do that?
I don't think that would work.
That's a good one!

COMMUNICATION ACTIVITY: HOW ABOUT SUNDAY?

Work in pairs. One of you should look at activity 32 and the other at activity 66. You are going to make plans with each other for the weekend by telephone. Sit back to back so that you can't see each other and will have to communicate by voice only.

Here are some popular sayings that deal with the weather.

When it rains, it pours.
It's raining cats and dogs.
April showers bring May flowers.
It's always darkest before the dawn.
Every cloud has a silver lining.
Don't rain on my parade.

Work in small groups or pairs and discuss what they mean.
a) Which ones are really about the weather?
b) Are there similar sayings in your country? Think of as many as you can in
   your group.
c) Discuss the English sayings and the sayings from your country with the rest
   of the class.

"It's raining cats and dogs."

5 Keep in touch

Your computer can connect you to the world

Using your telephone lines and your computer, you can get and send out more information than you ever believed possible – without ever leaving your living room!

JUST LOOK AT WHAT YOU CAN DO!

- GO SHOPPING
- DO YOUR BANKING
- GET UP-TO-DATE NEWS AND WEATHER REPORTS
- GET MOVIE REVIEWS
- GET INFORMATION ABOUT SPORTS
- READ TWO OR THREE NEWSPAPERS AND EVEN LOOK AT BACK ISSUES OF NEWSPAPERS

- DO RESEARCH IN HUNDREDS OF FIELDS WITHOUT EVER GOING INTO A LIBRARY
- GET FLIGHT SCHEDULES AND FARES, AND EVEN MAKE AIRLINE AND HOTEL RESERVATIONS
- SEND MESSAGES TO PEOPLE AND GET REPLIES
- PLAY A GAME OF CHESS WITH SOMEONE MILES AWAY

AND MUCH MORE

FOR MORE INFORMATION CALL **THE COMPUTER STORE** 962–0003 OR COME IN AND SEE US TODAY.

Discuss the following questions in class or in small groups.
a) Would you enjoy using a personal computer to do all these things or would you prefer to do things the way you always have?
b) If you had a personal computer, what would you like to use it for? Can you think of other things you could do with a personal computer?
c) Do you see personal computers as a positive force (adding another exciting aspect to life) or a negative one (making society impersonal) or perhaps both?
d) Are personal computers used a great deal in your country? For what purpose?
e) What are some other ways of communicating? Make a list. Here are some ideas to start you off: postcard, telephone...

Useful expressions

One thing I'd use it for is...　　*There's one computer system that...*
It would be great for...　　*I prefer/I'd rather communicate by...*

1. A secretary is taking phone messages for her boss, who is in a meeting. Listen to the first call and look at how the message was written down:

    Message #1

    > *Mary Roberts from First National Bank called. Please call her at 772-1852 before 12:30 or betw. 2 + 5 p.m. today.*

2. Now you will hear four more messages. Write them in the spaces below. Afterward, compare your messages with a partner's.

    Message #2

    Message #3

    Message #4

    Message #5

To_____	
Date_____	Time_____

    # WHILE YOU WERE OUT

    M_____

    of_____

    Phone_____ Message_____

    ☐ Telephoned   ☐ Called to see you   _____

    ☐ Please call   ☐ Wants to see you   _____

    ☐ URGENT   ☐ Will call again   _____

    ☐ Returned your call   _____

Useful expressions

I thought he said . . .   *No, he didn't say that. He said . . .*
Didn't she say something about . . . ?   *I didn't hear that, I heard . . .*
I didn't understand that part.   *Oh, yes. I think you're probably right.*

5.3   **COMMUNICATION ACTIVITY: MAY I SPEAK TO . . . ?**

Work in pairs. One of you should look at activity 26 and the other at
activity 64. You are going to have a telephone conversation with your
partner about an ad in the newspaper. Sit back to back so that you
can't see each other and will have to communicate by voice only.

5.4   **LISTENING ACTIVITY: GUESS WHAT I JUST HEARD!**

You are going to hear *one* side of four telephone conversations. Listen to the
recording and decide who each speaker is talking to and what he or she is talking
about. Afterward, compare your answers with a partner's.

Who is the speaker talking to?	Topic
1.	
2.	
3.	
4.	

Useful expressions

I think she was talking to . . .   *I'd really like to know . . .*
They seemed to be talking about . . .   *They were probably talking about . . .*
No, I don't think so. I think they were   *The most important clue was . . .*
  talking about . . .   *Maybe they were discussing . . .*

You are going to be telephoning for information on some adult education courses. Work with a partner. One of you should look at communication activity 31 and the other at activity 22. Sit back to back so that you can't see each other.

5.6

SHORT AND SWEET

These short telegrams were sent by people who wanted to save money. Work with a partner and try to figure out what each telegram is about. Notice that the telegrams in columns 2, 3, and 4 are all responses to the preceding telegram.

(1)	(2)	(3)	(4)
PASSED?	YES!	CONGRATULATIONS!	THANKS!
WHERE?	MY HOUSE!	WHEN?	MAY 6TH-8TH.
PLEASE!	NEVER!	WHY?	BECAUSE.
COMING?	SORRY, NO.	PLEASE!	OK.
ENGAGED!	WHEN?	APRIL 1ST.	HA! HA!

When you have decided what the telegrams mean, work with your partner and expand each one into a short telephone conversation.

Make up some other short telegrams and challenge another pair to figure them out. Then expand them into phone calls.

Useful expressions

I think the first person is saying that...
The other person just...
I think it has something to do with...

But why does he say...?
What do they mean by...?
I don't understand this one at all.

6 Once upon a time

LISTENING ACTIVITY: I REMEMBER...

1. Work in pairs. Ask each other what you remember most about
   - high school or college
   - your favorite or worst teacher
   - your first job
   - your best or worst school memory
   - your last day of school

Useful expressions

What do you remember about...?
Do you remember when (the first time you)...?
What's your most vivid memory of...?
Do you remember anything about...?

I especially remember...
Let me think just a minute...
The only thing I can remember is...
I'll never forget the time...

2. Some old friends are going to remember their days together in college. Listen to their conversation on the cassette, then fill in the chart below.

The way they looked
Grace:
Martin:
Curtis:
Their worst memory:
Their best memory:
Last day of college:

6.2 MEMORY LANE

Some people find it hard to remember what happened to them when they were younger. But if there is someone to jog your memory, it can be easy. Work in small groups and find out from your partners as much as you can about their

early childhood
birthdays and other celebrations
life when they were in school
vacations
first flight, train trip, trip abroad, drink, cigarette, date, interview, job, etc.

6.3 COMMUNICATION ACTIVITY: I'D REALLY LIKE TO KNOW...

Work with a partner. Imagine that you are going to write an article on either a famous actor or a famous politician. What would you like to know? Make a list of 10 questions that you think would be interesting. When you finish, one of you should look at activity 2 and the other at activity 29.

6.4 PEOPLE USED TO BELIEVE...

1. In the chart below you will find some things that people used to believe. Working with a partner, match each item in the first column with the correct answer in the second column, and make sentences.

People used to believe that...

tomatoes were...	foretold disaster.
the earth was...	fell faster than light ones.
comets...	flat.
heavy objects...	caused by evil spirits.
all illness was...	the center of the intelligence.
a woman's place was...	revolved around the earth.
the sun...	poisonous.
the heart was...	in the home.

2. Can you think of other things people used to believe?
3. Work with a partner and make a list of things you used to believe when you were younger, but that you don't believe anymore.

6.5 I'LL NEVER FORGET THE DAY I...

1. Begin alone. Can you remember a day in your life when everything seemed to go wrong? Try to remember the details and make a few notes. If you prefer, invent a story about yourself.
2. In groups, tell your stories. Then guess which stories really happened and which were invented.
3. Work alone again and try to remember the *best* day of your life, or invent a story of a happy day when everything went right.

4. In groups, tell your stories. Then guess which stories really happened and which were invented.

Useful expressions

It all started when . . .
I'll never forget the time I . . .
Everything went wrong/right.
And to make matters worse . . .

The worst/best was when . . .
I felt awful/great!
It was fabulous/terrible.

6.6   DETECTIVE WORK

Imagine that a man you know, Edward Johnson, suddenly disappears. He seemed happily married; he had two children and a good job in a bank. Everyone is baffled. Where is he? Did he leave on his own? If so, why? Was he kidnapped?

Work in groups. Look at the clues on the right and figure out what happened.

When you are ready, tell your version of the events to another group.

Useful expressions

He might have . . .
I think he probably . . .
But that doesn't make sense.
Maybe someone . . .
I don't think he was . . .
Our theory is that . . .

never want to see you again.
not try to get in touch with me
Jane

THE UNITED STATES OF
C 56820090 A
TEN DOLLAR

Best Travel, Inc. 4 Cedar St. . . . . .
BERKSHIRE TRAVEL AGENCY
2436 S. Main . . . . .
Brown's Travel Co. 13 W. 12th 4
CLUB MED
Over 3 million satisfied club members have vacationed at 100 Club Med villages worldwide
Reservations & Information
750–1670

CREATIVE TRAVEL S
1701 Airport Rd.
Comfort Travel Inc.
4500 South St. . . .
CORPORATE TRA
26 E. ota St.
vel Co. 13 N
St. . . . .
VEL SERVI

APOLLO THEATER
Evening
Thurs., Jan 15
8:00 p.m.
BALCONY

P 103

APOLLO THEATER
Evening
Thurs., Jan 15
8:00 p.m.
BALCONY

P 102

Notice of Terminat

o inform you that we
ur employment will be
as of January 9.

, your contract of em
weeks' notice of termination and
that your period of notice will
and end on Friday, January 9, 19

You will, of course, be entitled
termination, again as provided i
and a statement showing the tota
by which it is reached will be i
for days. Please return it to us

ACCOUNTS MANAGER

The International Bank is seeking an accounts manager for our new bank in Paris. The individual must have a minimum of 10 years' banking experience at the managerial level. Duties include setting sales and marketing policy, handling major accounts, and analyzing sales.

Excellent fringe benefits and salary. Applications are due by January 21

1. Work in pairs and discuss the Bayeux Tapestry, woven in the 11th century. What do these scenes from the tapestry tell you about the way people lived in those days?

Useful expressions

The (spears they carry) suggest that . . .   *They must have spent a lot of their*
It seems they used . . . to . . .   *time . . .*
They probably got (their food) by . . .

2. Imagine you could bury a time capsule containing 10 objects from the present day. What would you put inside? Choose things that would tell people 1,000 years from now what life is like today.
3. If you could go back in time to another era, what year would you choose? Why? Describe what you think life was like then.

6.8   **WORLD EVENTS**

Here are 10 historical events with the wrong dates on the left and the wrong places on the right. Can you match each date and place with the correct event?

1590	First book printed	U.S.A.
1938	First microscope	Holland
1455	First calculator	Britain
1926	Napoleon defeated	Belgium
1969	*Communist Manifesto* published	Denmark
1957	First tape recorder	France
1899	First TV	Germany
1642	First ballpoint pen	Hungary
1815	First artificial earth satellite	Britain
1848	First person on the moon	U.S.S.R.

1. These photographs were taken during this century. Work in pairs or small groups and decide which decade each comes from. What details of each photo tell you this?

2. Work in pairs or small groups. Choose *one* of the photos and imagine that you were the same age then as you are now. How do you think life was different in those days from the way it is now?

3. With a partner, discuss what changes have happened *in your own lifetime*. Think about the way people live and work, the things they eat and drink, how they travel, how they spend their spare time, and so on.

7 Staying home

LISTENING ACTIVITY: WHAT'S ON TV TONIGHT?

1. Decide with a partner which programs you'd like to watch together and mark them with an **X**. You have only *one* TV set.

TV GUIDE EVENING PROGRAMMING

7:00
(2) NEWS AND WEATHER
(4) TV MOVIE: "Women at West Point." Good drama about the first women to go to school at the top U.S. army academy.
(5) SPECIAL: "I Wanna Make Music." New videos by Madonna, Stevie Wonder, and David Bowie.
(7) MacFARLAN REPORTS. Nuclear power plants: How safe are they? Where are they being built?

7:30
(2) THE DATING GAME

8:00
(2) DETECTIVE: Private eye Jim Brown is called in to find a missing heiress.

(4) MOVIE: "Rocky IV." Rocky comes back to fight the Russian superfighter Drago.
(5) WORLD CUP SOCCER. Canada vs. Italy.
(7) THE CARVERS. Alexandra makes a fatal mistake.

9:00
(2) DYNASTY
(7) SPECIAL: "Psychology and You — Dreams." The most recent research on dreams.

10:00
(2) TV MOVIE: "Stranger Than Fiction." Documentary about amazing events and phenomena.
(4) CONSUMER REPORT: "Inexpensive vacations." How to travel almost anywhere in the world on a small budget.

10:30
(2) NEWS
(4) MOVIE: "High Plains Drifter." A Clint Eastwood western.
(5) BUSINESS WORLD: "Career Planning." A look at job opportunities in the future.

11:00
(2) MOVIE: "Kramer vs. Kramer." Dustin Hoffman and Meryl Streep in a drama about the breakup of a family.
(5) MOVIE: "Psycho." A classic Hitchcock thriller.
(7) NEWS

11:30
(7) THE TONIGHT SHOW. Host Johnny Carson welcomes guests Jane Fonda, Willie Nelson, and Julio Iglesias.

---

2. Listen to the recording. Two people are talking about the TV shows. Look at the TV guide as you listen and check off the programs the speakers are discussing.
3. Do you still want to watch the same shows or would you like to change your mind now? Discuss any changes with your partner and draw a circle around the programs you finally decide to watch.

Useful expressions

I'd really like to see . . .　　　　　　　　*Let's watch . . .*
That sounds good.　　　　　　　　　　*How about watching . . . ?*
I can't decide whether to . . .　　　　　*I hope you don't want to see . . .*
There's something good on Channel . . . at . . .　　*We can't watch both, so . . .*

DID YOU SEE . . . ?

The scenes on page 31 come from "Detective" (Channel 2 at 8:00 in the TV Guide). Work in pairs and decide what the story of the program was.
Tell your story to another pair and see if their story is the same as yours. If their story is different, how is it different?

Useful expressions

I think this picture shows . . .
This one probably shows . . .
What do you think happened in between?

What happened after that?
Yes, but why did he/she . . . ?
Is that the end of the story?

7.3   **LISTENING ACTIVITY: THEN WHAT HAPPENED?**

You're going to hear part of some of the programs in the TV guide on page 30. Unfortunately each program is interrupted so you don't hear the end.

1. Decide which program each recording comes from.

2. Talk to another student and work out how each program ended. What do you think each speaker said next?

Recording 1:
Recording 2:
Recording 3:
Recording 4:
Recording 5:

Useful expressions

It sounds like . . .
It could be . . .
It can't be . . .
Maybe she said . . .

What do you think came next?
I guess that after that . . .
The thing we don't know is . . .
I'll bet he . . .

Fill in this chart with the names of your favorites from your own country and from the rest of the world.

Your favorite	Your own country	International
TV show		
Actor		
Actress		
Movie (title)		
Book (title)		
Author		
Composer		
Singer		
Group or band		
Record		

Explain why some of these are your favorites. If your partners haven't heard of some of them, can you describe them?
How would you describe each of your national favorites to a foreigner?

Useful expressions

I think he's/she's/it's the best because . . .   *What kind of (book) is it?*
The reason he/she's so great is . . .   *What did he/she write?*
I can't think of a (composer).   *Oh, is he/she the one who . . . ?*
I've never heard of . . .   *He's OK, but I like . . . better because . . .*

Work in pairs. Imagine that you are talking on the phone to a friend. Sit back to back so that you can't see each other. One of you should look at activity 39 and the other at activity 55.

Work in pairs and talk about the hobbies you see here. What do you think is interesting or uninteresting about each one? Are they the kinds of things that interest you?

Some other hobbies are gardening, going to movies, listening to music, collecting records or cassettes, traveling, dancing, and astronomy. What are your hobbies? Explain why you enjoy them.

What hobbies did you have when you were younger? Why did you give some of them up?

Useful expressions

It must be fascinating to...   *That doesn't sound like much fun.*
I'd like to try that myself.   *If I had the time, I'd like to...*
I don't understand why people...   *I stopped..., because...*
It must take hours to...   *I used to..., but now I...*

Work in groups. Imagine that you have decided to invite everyone in your class, including your teacher, to a party at your place. Decide:

a) what kind of party you're going to have (costume, dancing, cocktail, dinner, etc.)
b) what each person should bring (records, drinks, food, decorations, etc.)
c) what each person's job is (to decorate, to pour drinks, to send invitations, to clean up, etc.)

Tell another group about the arrangements you have made.

8 Going out

1. Work in groups. Look at the entertainment section of the newspaper below. Discuss what your group would like to see together this evening, tomorrow evening, and the following evening.

2. Listen to the three conversations on the recording. Each pair is talking about their reaction to one of the events listed above. Decide which event they are describing and how much they liked it.
3. Now that you have heard the recording, does your group want to change its plans? Or do you want to keep your first choices?

8.2   COMMUNICATION ACTIVITY: CAN YOU TELL ME...?

Work in pairs. Telephone to get some information about one or more of the events in the newspaper above. Sit back to back so that you can't see each other. One of you should look at communication activity 6 and the other at activity 53.

These are eight scenes from the beginning, the middle, and the end of the same movie. Work in pairs and decide what happened in the movie. When you are ready, tell your story to another pair and listen to their story.

8.4 NIGHTLIFE

Fill in the questionnaire about your own evening activities.
Then work in pairs and find out what your partner likes to do in the evening.

How often do you go to:

the movies?_____   What kind of movies do you like?_____

the theater?_____   What shows or plays do you like?_____

the ballet or opera?_____   What is your favorite ballet or opera?_____

a concert?_____   What kinds of music do you like?_____

a bar or cafe?_____   What is your favorite bar or cafe?_____

a nightclub?_____   Which ones do you go to?_____

a place to dance?_____   What kind of dancing do you like best?_____

a restaurant?_____   What kind of food do you like most?_____

What other evening entertainment do you like?_____

Find out *why* your partner likes to do the things he or she does.
Stand up and go around the class, looking for people who like the same kind of entertainment that you do. Talk about the concerts you have seen, the places you have gone dancing, the movies that you have liked or disliked, and so on.

Useful expressions

Did you see . . . ?   *My favorite . . . is . . . because . . .*
Have you been to . . . ?   *Yeah, I like/liked it too.*
I like that kind of . . . too.   *Really? I like/liked . . . better.*
The best . . . I've seen in a long time was . . .

8.5 LET'S GET SOMETHING TO EAT!

1. Work in small groups. Imagine that you have arranged to meet and get something to eat. There are three good, inexpensive restaurants on the same street. Their menus are on the next page. Look at them and decide which one you want to go to. Take your time.

2. When you have decided which restaurant to go to, decide what each of you is going to order. Imagine that you all want to taste different dishes. Talk to your companions and decide on four or five dishes that all of you would like.

Bill's Burger Heaven

BURGERS

The Old Fashioned Hamburger
Served on a sesame seed bun with lettuce,
tomato, and pickle

Old-Fashioned
Cheeseburger

Mushroom Burger

Bacon Burger
Chili Burger
Onion Burger

All orders served with your choice of
French Fries, Baked Beans, Garden
Salad, or Cole Slaw

DESSERTS

Ice Cream   Apple Pie
Chocolate Cake   Chocolate Brownie

OTHER SPECIALTIES

Chili with Cheese or Sour Cream
Giant Grilled Hot Dogs
Chili Dogs

The Pizzeria

OLD FASHIONED PIZZA Small   Large

Your choice of toppings: Medium

Pepperoni	Sausage
Onions	Meatballs
Green Peppers	Olives
Mushrooms	Anchovies

VEGETARIAN PIZZA

Cheese with Green Onion
Mushroom, Onion, and Green Pepper
Broccoli and Garlic

SALAD

Lettuce and Tomato

HOT SANDWICHES

Meatball
Sausage
Sausage and Pepper
Cheese steak

around the world

APPETIZERS

New England Clam
  Chowder
Feta Cheese with Olives

Tortilla Chips with
  Avocado Dip
Mushroom Paté

MAIN DISHES

Vegetable Tempura
Southern Fried Chicken
Shrimp Creole
Veal with Cream and
  Mushrooms
Sausage and Sauerkraut
Texas Barbeque - Beef Ribs

Spaghetti with Tomato
  Sauce
African Peanut Stew
Chicken Curry
Sweet and Sour Shrimp
Shish Kebab

All main dishes include salad and a choice of two
  vegetables:

Baked or Home-Fried
  Potatoes
French Green Beans
Eggplant Parmesan

Artichokes with Dill
  Sauce
All-American Cole Slaw

DESSERTS

Pecan Pie
Cream Puff
Baklava

Italian Lemon Ice
Chinese Fried Bananas

Useful expressions

I'd like to have the . . .
That sounds good.
I can't eat . . .
I'll get the . . . if you'll get the . . .

I don't care for . . .
I can't stand . . .
Let's try the . . .

8.6   COMMUNICATION ACTIVITY: ARE YOU READY TO ORDER?

Choose one person in your group to be the waiter or waitress. The others will order
what they want to eat from the appropriate menu above. The waiter or waitress
should look at communication activity 35 and all the others should look at activity 80.

9 One of these days

AS TIME GOES BY

Work with a partner. Imagine that these children live in your country or the country you come from.
a) What kind of future do you think they will have?
b) What will life be like for them when they are your age?
c) How will life be different for the boy and for the girl?
d) If you and your partner are from different countries, talk about how the lives of the children would be different in the two countries.

e) Do you wish you were their age and could look forward to the same future?
f) How would you change your life if you were their age again?

Useful expressions

They'll probably have to/be able to . . .   *It'll be harder/easier for him/her . . .*
They won't have to/be able to . . .   *It may be more . . .*
They'll have . . .   *If I were/could . . . , I would . . .*

9.2   **CHANGES**

---

1. Work in groups and discuss the following questions. Talk about what you *hope* will happen and what you think will *really* happen 5 years from now and 20 years from now.
   a) How will life be different?
   b) Where will you be living?
   c) What kind of house/apartment will you be living in?
   d) What will you be doing?
   e) Will you be married? Have children?
   f) What will you do on a typical day?
   g) What sort of transportation will you use?
   h) How will you spend your spare time?

2. Do you think prices will go up or down in the future? Discuss in groups how much you think the following items will cost 5 years from now.

a gallon (or liter) of gasoline	an ice cream cone	a cup of coffee at a cafe
a daily newspaper	local bus fare	a movie ticket
a pair of jeans	a personal computer	a new car
a pair of running shoes	a can of soda	

3. The following events might happen one day. Work with a partner and put them in order according to which you think will happen sooner. Which do you think will never happen?

DRUGS TO CURE COLDS   **THREE-DAY WEEK FOR ALL**   **Picturephones in every home**

SALARIES FOR ALL HOUSEWIVES   The U.S.S.R. and the U.S.A. become allies

FREE PUBLIC TRANSPORTATION   **Communication with intelligent life in Space**

Credit cards replace money entirely   **South Africa ends Apartheid**

Add two events you would like to see happen during your own lifetime.

9.3   LISTENING ACTIVITY: A VISION OF THE FUTURE

1. Listen to the cassette about the science fiction movie *Soylent Green*.

2. Read the questions below. Listen to the recording again and take notes. Then work with a partner and answer the questions.
   a) Which of the following are in short supply or no longer exist in 2022?
      apartments   water   soybeans
      soil   soap   fuel
      lettuce   beef   ocean plants
   b) What is the percentage of unemployment?
      20%   30%   50%   75%
   c) What is the weather like?
   d) What do people eat? What is it made of?
   e) Which of the two people talking is the more optimistic about the future?
   f) After you have listened to the recording and answered the questions, get together in groups and discuss whether the future described in *Soylent Green* is possible. How close are we to such a future? Can we prevent it? Will we? How do you foresee the future?

3. Find out if any of your partners can tell you about another movie or book about life in the future.

9.4 COMMUNICATION ACTIVITY: WHAT'S IN YOUR FUTURE?

You are going to have your fortune told.
Work with a partner. One of you should look
at activity 76 and the other at activity 7.

9.5 THE TIME MACHINE

1. Work in pairs. Imagine that you are going on a trip that will take you 100 years
into the future. What will you need when you arrive? You have only enough room
in your time machine for some of the equipment listed below, but not all. Put each
item into one of these categories:

ABSOLUTELY ESSENTIAL

USEFUL BUT NOT ESSENTIAL

NO USE AT ALL

aspirin	checkbook	food
bicycle	Chinese phrase book	Russian dictionary
notebooks	heavy shoes	sleeping bag
camera	English dictionary	raincoat
car	television set	radio
cash	sunglasses	watch
warm clothes	tape recorder	calculator

2. Are there any absolutely essential items that aren't on the list? Think of three and
write them down. Then get together with another pair and compare your lists. If
you could take only *two* items, which ones would you take?

3. Your time machine can travel only in time, not space, so it will take you to the
place you are in now. Work with a partner and decide what changes you expect to
see 100 years from now. After 24 hours the time machine is programmed to
return. What will you do during your one day in the future?

Useful expressions

I don't think we'll need . . .
I'd certainly like to take . . .
Why would you need a . . . ?
I'd take . . . just in case . . .

Another thing we'll need is . . .
What about a . . . ?
A . . . would be useless.
Maybe . . . would come in handy.

The tropical island state of Boa Boa lies in the center of the Pacific Ocean, close to the equator. Its climate is pleasant. Until now the 200,000 islanders have lived from fishing, agriculture, and a little tourism. Half the population lives in small villages on the north and south coasts; the other half lives in the three main towns. The capital city is Topa. Now that oil has been discovered off the east coast of the island, the government wants to make Boa Boa into the "best of all possible worlds."

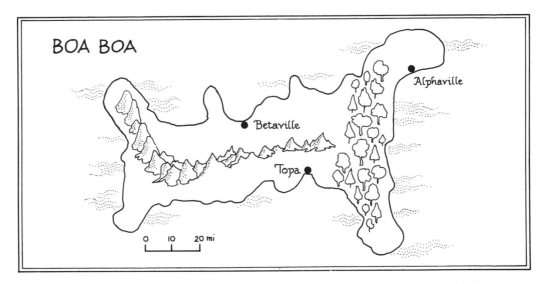

Work as 3 committees. Each committee will discuss a different aspect of the island's future, and produce a report. Committee A should look at activity 16, committee B at activity 38, and committee C at activity 85.

10 Staying healthy

GETTING IN SHAPE

Many large companies have exercise programs for their employees. Here are three Xerox employees working out.

Work with a partner and discuss the following questions:
a) What seems to be the purpose of each of these machines?
b) Do you think companies should provide exercise programs?
c) Should people be allowed to take time off from work to exercise?
d) How does it help a company if its employees are in good physical condition?
e) What kind of exercises do you do to stay in shape?
f) What else do you do to stay healthy?

1. Work in pairs. These people have problems, but they aren't seriously ill. If they were friends of yours, what advice would you give them?
    For example: *If you get a black eye, you should . . . and you shouldn't . . .*
    If you have a fever, you should . . . and you shouldn't . . .

2. Listen to the recording. Write down what is wrong with each person, and then write down in the table below the advice he or she receives.

	Problem	*Advice*
First person		
Second person		
Third person		
Fourth person		

10.3   **COMMUNICATION ACTIVITY: WHAT WOULD YOU DO IF . . . ?**

Work with a partner. You are going to be giving each other some advice on how to feel better. One of you should look at communication activity 28 and the other at activity 3.

1. Each of the people in these pictures is doing something that can be dangerous or unhealthy. Work with a partner and explain the dangers in each cartoon. What *shouldn't* each of the people be doing?

2. Which of these activities do you think is the most dangerous? Number the cartoons with the most dangerous activity first and the least dangerous last.
3. Are you someone who "plays safe" and tries to be careful, or do you usually trust to luck?

The Big Burger Company wants to open a new hamburger restaurant. Work in groups of four. Two of you should look at activity 44 and the other two at activity 60.

11　It's all in a day's work

1. You're going to hear four people talking about their jobs. Listen to each recording and fill in the missing information. Compare your answers with the class.

a) His job:
   Why he likes it:
   Why he doesn't like it:

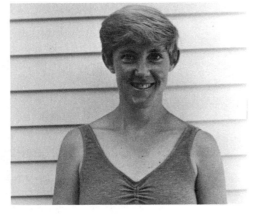

b) Her job:
   Why she likes it:
   Why she doesn't like it:

c) His job:
   Why he likes it:
   Why he doesn't like it:

d) Her job:
   Why she likes it:
   Why she doesn't like it:

2. Work in pairs or small groups. Describe your own typical work day or describe a typical work day of a friend or family member.

In a recent survey, people were asked what they enjoyed the most about their work and what gave them the most satisfaction. Here are some of their comments:

"The pay is good."   "I'm my own boss."
"I get long vacations."   "The people I work with are great."
"I enjoy the responsibility."   "I get to travel a lot."
"There are a lot of opportunities for   "I like meeting people."
    promotion."   "I don't like responsibility, and there isn't
"I like making decisions."   much of it in this job."
"I like working alone."

1. Which things are most important for *you* in a job? Which are not important for you? Make a list of the three most important and the three least important things.
2. Discuss your choices in small groups. Did the discussion make you want to change your list?
3. Work with a partner. Discuss the advantages and disadvantages of having to work for a living.

Useful expressions

I think it's important . . .   *The best/worst things about my job are . . .*
I like being able to . . .   *I hate having to . . .*
It doesn't really matter if . . .   *I'd rather have a job that . . .*

1. Work in pairs and rank these jobs according to how well-paid you think they are in the United States.

electrician   chemical engineer   nurse
flight attendant   firefighter   police officer
accountant   doctor   teacher (primary school)
bus driver (big city)   mail carrier   lawyer
computer systems analyst   plumber

1. _____   8. _____

2. _____   9. _____

3. _____   10. _____

4. _____   11. _____

5. _____   12. _____

6. _____   13. _____

7. _____   14. _____

When you finish, look at activity 82, and see how these jobs were ranked according to the *Occupational Outlook Handbook, 1984–1985*.

2. Work in pairs and discuss these questions:
   a) Which of these jobs do you think are the most boring? the most interesting?
   b) Can you think of some other jobs that are particularly exciting, dangerous, or unpleasant?
   c) Are there jobs that men do better than women, and vice versa?
   d) How do you think these jobs would rank for pay in your own country?
   e) Nurses and teachers have to study longer than bus drivers, mail carriers, and police officers. Why do you think they earn less money?

11.4   PUT YOURSELF IN MY SHOES

1. Work in pairs and discuss the qualities of a good student and a good teacher. Here are some comments from an opinion poll. Check off the ones that you think are appropriate qualities, and add more qualities to the list.

A good student
Always comes to class on time
Memorizes the book
Asks the teacher a lot of questions
Always does the homework
Listens quietly to the teacher and takes a lot of notes
Tries to figure out problems without help

_____

_____

_____

A good teacher
Is very friendly with students
Is very strict
Tells students everything they need to learn
Asks students to give their ideas
Makes students figure out problems for themselves
Always knows the answers to the students' questions

_____

_____

_____

2. Work in pairs and discuss the advantages and disadvantages of being a teacher. Make a list and read it to the class. Do they agree with you? Does your teacher agree?
3. Work in pairs and discuss the qualities you need to do your job well. Make a list of the qualities like the one in number 1. If you aren't working now, talk about a job you would like to have.

47

1. Work in pairs. Look at these pictures and decide what each person's job is. Choose one of them and try to imagine what he or she does on a typical day at work. What are the best things about the job? What are some of the problems? Try to put yourself in their shoes. How would you like doing their jobs?

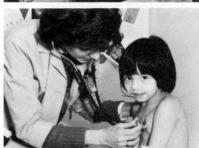  

2. After you have described all the people, choose one and describe that person's typical work day to another pair.

11.6   **COMMUNICATION ACTIVITY: JOB INTERVIEW**

Read this help-wanted ad. Half the class will pretend they are applying for the job. The other half will interview them.

HOTEL

Assistant Manager

Luxury hotel needs hard-working, ambitious individual for assistant night manager position. Must have pleasant manner and ability to deal with people and solve problems quickly. Excellent working conditions, benefits, and career opportunities. Varied and interesting duties, lots of contact with people.

Must type 60 words per minute. General bookkeeping and managerial skills a plus. Hotels in 5 countries – opportunity for future transfer. Send résumé to Box 79024, Chicago, IL 60680.

The job applicants should turn to communication activity 73, and the interviewers to activity 48.

12 Getting away from it all

WHAT A GREAT VACATION!

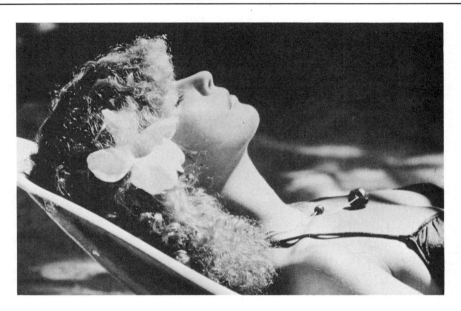

1. Work in pairs. Tell your partner what your idea of a great summer vacation is. Look at the following suggestions for places and activities, and add others of your own.

   TYPE OF PLACE
   the mountains   Other: _____
   the beach
   a big city
   a small town   _____
   a resort
   the jungle   _____
   an out-of-the-way hotel or resort

   ACTIVITIES
   sports – walking, bicycling, boating, swimming,   visiting friends
     sailing, water skiing, snorkeling, hiking,   camping – fishing, hunting
     tennis, volleyball, golf   doing nothing
   shopping
   sightseeing – museums, historic monuments   Other: _____
     and buildings, natural wonders
   relaxing – lying on the beach, reading   _____
   socializing – dancing, going to nightclubs and
     restaurants   _____

2. Tell your partner about the best vacation you have ever had. What made it so much fun? What was your worst vacation? Why was it so awful?

1. Look at the departure board and listen to the recording. Fill in the missing information. Listen to the tape as many times as necessary to get all the information.

DEPARTURES					
Airline	*Flight number*	*Destination*	*Departure time*	*Status of flight*	*Gate*
KLM	330	London/Amsterdam	2:15	On time	15
Aeromexico			2:30		
Japan Air Lines			2:35	Now boarding	
		Vancouver	2:15		
Pan Am				Delayed	26
	224			Cancelled	

2. Work in pairs and check the information you wrote down in your departure boards. Did you both write down the same information?

Useful expressions

Yes. That's what I have too.   *I thought she said . . .*
I didn't hear that. I heard . . .   *It sounded like . . . to me.*

1. In pairs or groups look at the photographs and try to figure out where in the world each place is.
2. Put the places in order according to how much you would like to visit each one of them.
3. Tell your partner what other places in the world you would like to visit and explain why.

1. Listen to the recording of a young man talking with a travel agent about the best way to travel from Paris to Frankfurt. Make notes in the table below.

	Cost	Advantages	Disadvantages
Plane			
Train			
Car			
Bus			

2. Now work with a partner and decide which way to go to Frankfurt. When you have decided, report to the class and explain the reasons for your choice.

Useful expressions

I'd rather go by . . . because . . .
But if we take the plane . . .
Why don't we take the . . . ?

12.5   COMMUNICATION ACTIVITY: SOMEPLACE DIFFERENT

Work in groups of three. Imagine that each of you has heard something about the following places:

PARADISE ISLAND   HIDDEN BEACH   PORTO ADRIANO

A vacation in each place costs about the same. Decide where you should go. For more information, one of you should look at communication activity 63, one at activity 23, and the other at activity 79.

Imagine that you took the same vacation as the people in the picture. You either loved every minute of it *or* you hated every minute of it. Work in pairs and make up a story of your vacation. When you are ready, get together with another pair and tell them about your vacation.

12.7   **COMMUNICATION ACTIVITY: HOW DO I GET THERE?**

Work in pairs. Imagine that one of you lives in Rockwood and the other is a tourist who has just arrived in town. One of you should look at activity 59 and the other at activity 33.

"EXCUSE ME, I DON'T UNDERSTAND"

Each of the phrases below means: "I don't understand. Do you speak English?"
Can you match the phrase to the languages on the right? Work in pairs.

Jeg forstar ikke. Taler De engelsk?	Mandarin Chinese
En puhu. Puhuetteko englantia?	Swahili
Dhen katalaveno. Milate anglika?	Spanish
Wǒ bù dǒng. Nǐ huì shūo Yīngwén ma?	Danish
Je ne comprends pas. Parlez-vous anglais?	Portuguese
Ja nie rozumiem po. Czy pan mówi po angielsku?	Japanese
Sifahamu. Unasema Kingereza?	Italian
No entiendo. ¿Habla inglés?	German
Ich verstehe nicht. Sprechen Sie Englisch?	French
Não compreendo. Fala inglês?	Finnish
Non capisco. Parla inglese?	Greek
Wakarimasen. Eigo o hanasemasuka?	Polish

If you need some clues, one of you can look at activity 69, while the other looks at
activity 45.

12.9   **AROUND THE WORLD**

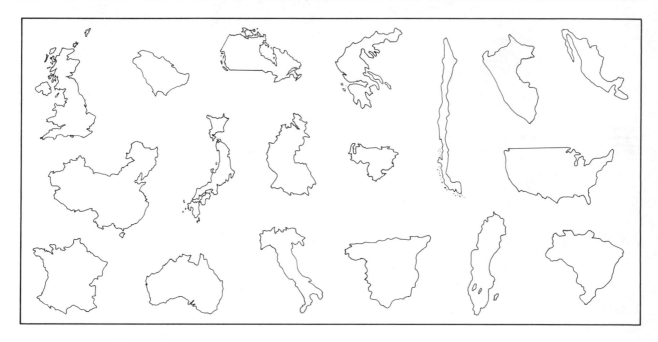

1. Work in pairs and try to name the countries shown above. (They are not drawn to
   the same scale.) If absolutely necessary, you can look at communication activity
   10, where all the countries are listed – but you'll still have to identify which is
   which from their shapes!
2. What do you call a person who comes from each of these countries? What language or languages do they speak there? If you need help, ask another pair.

13 In the news

13.1 LISTENING ACTIVITY: THE 5 O'CLOCK NEWS

Listen to the four newscasts and decide whether the following statements are true or false.

a) The town of Delta was poisoned by toxic wastes leaking into the water and soil.
A game of football in the park could be dangerous to the residents' health.
The residents have to stay indoors until the town has been cleaned up.

b) A recent study showed that 17,000 Canadians drink alcoholic beverages.
People who drink beer once or twice a day don't get sick as often as people who drink wine and liquor.
People who drink 35 pints or more of beer a week are the healthiest of all.

c) Legislation has been introduced that would make smoking illegal.
Under this legislation, a cigarette company would not be allowed to sponsor the New York City marathon.
Studies have shown that prohibiting the advertising of cigarettes has caused a decrease in cigarette smoking.

d) Mexico had an easy win over France.
Haiti lost to Italy by one goal.

13.2 HEADLINES

Work with a partner and figure out what each of these headlines means.
Which articles do you think you would like to read?
Why?

Computer translates language perfectly – Language teachers now unemployed

CURE FOR BALDNESS DISCOVERED

Robots go on strike, humans get jobs back

New country discovered in South Pacific

PILOTS MOVE LUGGAGE

Scientists discover way to reverse aging

Planet Earth declared toxic: pioneer flights begin to Mars

Study shows that Government employees work only 2 hours a day

Work in small groups, and write a caption for each of these news photos.

Talk about what's happening in each picture.
What makes a good news photograph? Which of the ones
above is the best? Which is the worst?
Why do you think so?

Find an interesting news photograph from a newspaper
and cut it out. Can your partners remember or imagine what is
happening in the photo?

Add speech or thought bubbles to your photograph to show
what the people in it might be saying or thinking.

Look at these cartoons
from the opinion page of
a newspaper. Work in
small groups.
What do the drawings in
each cartoon represent?
What message is the
cartoon trying to get across?
Do you agree
or disagree?

You are going to be interviewed by a roving reporter. Half the class should look at
activity 49 and the other half at activity 57.

Read the following newspaper article.

Beth Marinelli is 29 years old, 5 feet 4 inches tall – and approximately 350 pounds. She is not always able to fit herself into theater or restaurant seats, or into train or airplane seats. She has to go to specialty stores to buy clothes. All of this angers Beth Marinelli. But what angers her most is New Jersey's mandatory seat belt law.

New Jersey drivers and front seat passengers are required by law to wear seat belts. The problem for Beth Marinelli is that car manufacturers don't make seat belts large enough for obese people. As a result, people with weight problems are not required to buckle up like everybody else. "Statistics show how much safer it is to be in an accident while wearing a seat belt," says Marinelli. "The lawmakers are saying that if you're fat, you can be exempt from wearing a seat belt – that it's OK to die in a car accident."

Marinelli talks publicly about the obese who face discrimination and has formed a group called HOPE – Helping Oversized People Everywhere. But this is only one step in her attempt to get the same opportunities for overweight people as for "normal" people.

"I want them to change the anti-discrimination laws from 'You can't discriminate on the basis of race, creed, color, or sex,' to 'You can't discriminate on the basis of race, creed, color, sex, or weight,'" says Marinelli. She claims that she is forced to work as a cook at her brother's fast food restaurant because her weight discourages employers from hiring her.

Social discrimination against the obese is very strong, according to Marinelli. She left high school because of constant teasing about her weight. But the cruel jokes and comments didn't end with her youth. She recalls being out on a date with a young man and overhearing a woman say to a friend: "What is that beautiful man doing with that fat cow?"

One day Marinelli wants to write a book about her life. She'll call it

"Growing Up Fat in America." She wants to warn young people who are overweight about what's in store for them, and encourage them to lose weight. "If one 10-year-old fat kid listens to me and says, 'I don't want to go through that,' then I've succeeded."

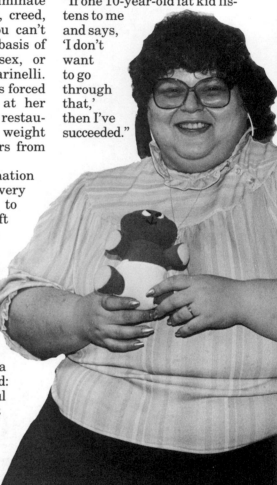

In small groups, discuss the following questions.
a) What are the difficulties that fat people have? Can you think of others not mentioned in the article?
b) What do you think about Marinelli's "fat rights" crusade?
c) List some other minorities who are victims of discrimination and describe their problems. (examples: left-handed people, very tall people, handicapped people)
d) What should be done, if anything, to accommodate these "special" people?
e) Are these problems similar to the discrimination problems faced by women, races, or religious groups? Explain why or why not.

Work in small groups. Imagine that the whole world is ruled by one government and that you and your partners are leaders in that government.

It isn't in your power to change human nature, but you can try to improve social life and economic affairs.
What *five* changes would you propose?

Write down your proposals. Then explain them to another group of leaders.

Useful expressions

I think I'd . . .
The first thing I'd want to do is . . .
If possible, I'd . . .

14   I don't agree

14.1   **PROTEST**

---

1. Read the following newspaper article and, working with a partner, write what you think each person said.

Protest gets nasty – 41 arrested

by Birney Jarvis

About 200 anti-war demonstrators went wild yesterday, invading stores, knocking down pedestrians, and breaking windows before police moved in to arrest them.

The problem began when a small group of punk rockers, "skinheads," admitted anarchists, and students ran into one of the department stores at Post and Powell streets at 6 p.m. pushing and shoving customers. Some were knocked down, witnesses said.

Within seconds, several squads of police in riot gear and 30 motorcycle officers and mounted police moved in. A total of 41 people were arrested.

The Police Commander, Ray Canepa, said ....

....

....

....

....

....

....

A store owner on Powell Street said ....

....

....

....

....

One of the protesters, a high school student at Concord High, said ....

....

....

....

....

and one of the customers who was pushed around by the rioters said ....

....

....

The mayor, who came down to the scene of he riot, said ....

....

....

....

....

....

....

....

....

....

2. Discuss the following questions with a partner:
   a) How do you feel about demonstrations? Do they help a cause? How?
   b) Can a demonstration hurt a cause? How?
   c) Do you think the demonstration in the article helped the anti-war cause? Why or why not?

Useful expressions

People have a right to . . .
If you want to get publicity for a cause, . . .

I think a demonstration can do some good if . . .
Demonstrations don't help because . . .

14.2   LISTENING ACTIVITY: I DON'T SEE IT THAT WAY

Work with a partner. You are going to hear three different conversations. Write down what the people are arguing about in each one. Then write down the arguments for each side.

	Conflict	*Arguments*	
1.		Customer's side:	Clerk's side:
2.		Husband's side:	Wife's side:
3.		Employee's side:	Boss's side:

Who do you think is right in each discussion? Why? Who do you think "won" each argument?

14.3 COMMUNICATION ACTIVITY: DISAGREEMENTS

Work with a partner. You are going to complain to each other about different things. One of you should look at activity 71 and the other at activity 17.

14.4 WHAT DO YOU THINK?

1. Read the following item from the newspaper.

What do you think?

TODAY'S QUESTION: A recent study concluded that the world's population will double to 10 billion by 2050. Do you think enough food can be produced to feed all of these people?

Annette Vale   25

I think there will be plenty to eat in 2050. Scientists are discovering new foods and better ways to produce food every day. I think we'll have better fertilizer and we'll grow more corn, rice, and wheat than ever before. Also new sources of food will be discovered. In 2050 we will probably be eating things we never dreamed of eating today.

Pete Jordan   20

I think it will be possible to feed everyone, but only if we stop spending millions of dollars to go into space, to build armies, and to make bigger and more destructive weapons. We have to start using that money for research on farming. Also, if we change the way we eat, we can use our land more efficiently. If, for example, we used farms to grow grains to feed people instead of animals, we could feed a lot more people. We need to rely less on animals for food and more on grains, fruits, and vegetables.

Dave Vargas   45

I'm just glad I won't be around then. I think thousands of people are going to starve to death. People will probably have to eat things like bugs, too. I mean, just look at the world today. People are already starving in a lot of places.

What do you think?

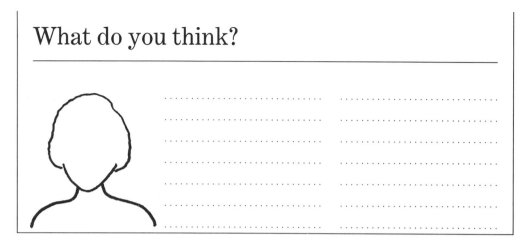

2. Work in groups and discuss the following questions.
   a) Do you think it's possible for everyone in the world to have enough to eat? Why or why not?
   b) What would have to be done in order to feed everyone?
   c) Do you think the people and the governments of the world will do what is necessary to produce enough food in the future?

14.5   LISTENING ACTIVITY: CAPITAL PUNISHMENT

1. Listen to two friends arguing about capital punishment. The first time you listen, decide which person you agree with. The next time you listen, write down the reasons that person gives to explain her position.

Reasons:

2. Find a partner who feels the same way you do about capital punishment. Compare your notes with his or hers. Then try to think of some other reasons to support your position. Include them in the list.
3. With your partner, decide which reason is the most important. Put a 1 next to the most important, a 2 next to the second most important, and so on.
4. Find two people who don't agree with you and your partner. Explain to them why you feel the way you do.

1. Below are some arguments for and against smoking in public places. Work in groups of four. Read the arguments.
2. Divide into pairs. Two of you will argue for smoking in public and two of you against. Work with your partner and prepare your argument, using your own ideas and perhaps the ideas here.
3. Try to convince the other two people in your group that you are right.

FOR
— There is no real proof that smoke is harmful to nonsmokers.
— People who are allergic to smoke can avoid places where people smoke just like people who are allergic to cats avoid places where there are cats.
— Smokers have rights to enjoy what they like to do. Lots of annoying activities aren't banned in public.
— To ban smoking in restaurants would prevent smokers from enjoying the meal.

AGAINST
— Smoking is bad for the health of smokers *and* nonsmokers.
— Nonsmokers find smoke irritating to their eyes, nose, and throat, and they don't like the smell.
— Smokers litter.
— In restaurants, smoke spoils the taste of food and spoils the meal.

Is it possible to guess what a person thinks by the way he or she looks?

Work in groups. Do you think these two people have similar or different opinions about most things?

Decide what each one would say about
– rock music
– clothing
– what to do for a fun night out
– how to decorate an apartment
– the kind of job he would like
– the military
– making money
– raising children
– hunger in the world
– nuclear war
– what's important in life

What are some other subjects that these two people might agree or disagree about?

Useful expressions

I think he would say . . .   *I don't think he'd like . . .*
He'd probably want to . . .   *He would probably . . . , but he wouldn't . . .*

1. Here are six well-known political sayings. Work in pairs and decide which of the men below first used each saying.

    "Man is born free, but everywhere he is in chains."
    "From each according to his ability, to each according to his needs."
    "All we are saying is give peace a chance."
    "All men are created equal."
    "Government of the people, for the people and by the people."
    "In this life nothing can be said to be certain, except death and taxes."

    Thomas Jefferson (1743–1826), U.S. President
    Benjamin Franklin (1706–1790), U.S. statesman
    John Lennon (1940–1980), British musician
    Karl Marx (1818–1883), German political philosopher
    Jean Jacques Rousseau (1712–1778), French philosopher and author
    Abraham Lincoln (1809–1865), U.S. President

    (You can find the right answers in activity 34, but don't look there until you've matched up each saying with a person.)

2. In small groups, discuss which of the sayings you believe in. Which do you disagree with? Can you think of any other well-known political sayings?

15 The persuaders

15.1 COME FLY WITH ME

From the people who invented civilization:
A more civilized way to fly.

At Olympic, the international airline of Greece, we've taken a leaf out of our ancestors' book.

Like them, we believe that life was meant to be better. So on Olympic flights, you'll find the seats a little more comfortable than usual.

The flight smoother and quieter than you'd expect. And the food fit for heroes. (Who knows more what heroes like to eat than the Greeks?)

Have you had the Olympic experience recently? It really is a more civilized way to fly.

OLYMPIC
A I R W A Y S
A more civilized way to fly.

"Lufthansa's technical success is due, first of all, to the airline's highly progressive fleet-management."
Le Monde (Paris), 2. 2. 81

Because our planes are new we can offer you cleaner, quieter, more comfortable flights. We can also offer you a punctuality record that is second to none wherever you fly in the world.

 Lufthansa
German Airlines

Discuss the following questions with a partner:
a) If you could choose to fly somewhere on one of these airlines *or* on your own national airline, which would you choose? Why?
b) Which of the three advertisements appeals to you the most and which the least? Why?
c) What are the qualities of a good magazine or newspaper ad? of a good TV commercial?

Useful expressions

It gets your attention.
It gives you good reasons to use a product.
It makes . . . look or sound better than . . .
It's funny.
It makes you think . . .

Cut out a good ad and a bad ad from a newspaper or magazine. Explain to your partner why you chose them.

NOW FLY JAL

Serving you is our way. JAL

How do we serve you? Let us begin to count the ways: we serve with a joyous heritage of service that dates back over a thousand years, with meals that please the eye as well as the palate, with the best 747 on-time record in the world, with reservations that are quick and accurate, with mechanics who not only meet the high standards of the industry but the more exacting requirements of JAL itself. There are over 20,000 of us around the world. To us, serving you is more than a job, **serving you is our way.**

JAPAN AIR LINES

1. What are some products or services that are advertised on TV or on the radio where you live? Tell your partner about some commercials you remember.
2. Listen to the three recordings and decide what each radio commercial is trying to sell.

	Name of company	Type of product or service
1.		
2.		
3.		

3. Which of the commercials was the best? Why?

15.3   **COMMUNICATION ACTIVITY: YOU TALKED ME INTO IT!**

Work in groups of 4. You are going to become salespeople. Two of you should look at activity 24 and two at activity 5. Decide together how you are going to sell your product. Then try to sell it to the other two people in your group.

15.4   **FIRST IMPRESSIONS**

Each of these pictures is part of an advertisement.
Work with a partner and try to decide what each is advertising.
When you have decided,
  look at activity 88.
Now that you know
  what the ads are
  selling, how effective
  do they seem to you?
Why?

15.5   BRAINSTORMING

Imagine that you work for an advertising agency and you have been asked to organize a campaign to sell a new brand of one of the following:

BEER   DETERGENT   CAT FOOD   INSTANT COFFEE

Work in pairs and:
1. Decide what type of people will probably buy your product so you will know how to orient your ad.
2. Find a suitable name for the product.
3. Decide whether you want to advertise in the newspaper, in magazines, on TV, or on radio.
4. Invent some good slogans for the product and sketch out an ad or write an outline for a commercial.

Work with another pair and imagine they are your clients. Explain your ad campaign to them.

15.6   BOOK OF THE YEAR

Work with a partner and prepare a poster or advertisement persuading people to buy this book.

Show your work to the rest of the class and decide whose ad is the best.

Communication activities

You need to take a business trip in June to one or more of these places:

Mexico City, Mexico   Vancouver, Canada
Madrid, Spain   Buenos Aires, Argentina

Go to your travel agent and ask about the weather there and what kind of clothes you should take.

Useful expressions

What will the weather be like in . . . ?   *Does it rain that time of year?*
Do you think I'll need . . . ?   *Is it OK to wear . . . ?*
Will it get cold at night?

After you have gotten all the information you need about what clothes to take, look at activity 70.

1

You have been assigned to write a short biography (about 10–15 lines) of the famous actress Marilyn Monroe. Decide what you want to know and ask your partner questions. Take notes of the answers. Afterward, write your report. You may be asked to present it to the rest of the class.

When you have finished, look at activity 78.

2

Your partner isn't feeling well. Listen to what is wrong with him or her and then offer some advice. If you don't know what advice to give, ask another pair to help you.

Useful expressions

What's wrong?   *Don't you think you should . . . ?*
That's too bad.   *Have you tried . . . ?*
Why don't you . . . ?   *. . . always works for me.*

When you have finished, look at activity 51.

3

4

You are a reporter for radio station QXBK, and you have been assigned to stop people on the street and ask them questions for a survey. Introduce yourself and ask your partner these questions.

1. What's your name? Where are you from?
2. What's the best thing that has happened to you recently?
3. What's your favorite way to relax?
4. What would you like to be doing five years from now?
5. If you could change places with anyone in the world, who would you become? Why?

When you have finished, thank your partner for participating in the survey, and look at activity 9.

5

Read the following ad. Work with a partner and think of good reasons to own this product. Then try to convince the other two people in your group to get it.

Introducing
The Smallest Color Television — By Seiko
$269.50

This color television is small enough to carry in your hand or fit in your pocket. The 2-inch diagonal screen is virtually unbreakable, making this TV ideal for travel and recreational use. AC or DC operation; runs on batteries (included). Height: 3 1/8 inches. Width: 6 3/8 inches. Depth: 1 1/4 inches. Weight (with batteries): 1 pound.

When you have finished, turn to activity 65.

6

You want to go to one or more of the movies on page 34. Telephone the theaters where they are playing and get some information about the movie.

Useful expressions

What times is . . . showing? *How much are the tickets?*
When does . . . start?   *What's the address of the theater?*
When does the show get out?

When you have finished, look at activity 77.

You are going to read the future. Your partner will tell you his or her astrological sign. Using the information below, tell your partner his or her future. Feel free to invent information of your own to make the prediction more interesting.
Your partner will tell you the astrological sign of some other people. Tell their future too.

7

ARIES
You will have important decisions to make this year. Don't make any big changes. The job and relationship that you are in now are good for you. Work to make them better.

TAURUS
You may start seeing an old love again. Be careful with your money. Save some – you're going to need it for something unexpected.

GEMINI
There will be a lot of changes this year, and most of them will be good for you. Don't look back. This is a time to move forward, make new friends, start a new job, begin new activities.

CANCER
You are going to feel very creative and self-confident this year. There are some surprises ahead, perhaps a new love. A phone call could change your life.

LEO
Family member could give you trouble. Control your temper. You'll be invited to a very elegant dinner and could receive a very special honor. This is a good year for travel.

VIRGO
Stop being so critical. Accept friend's apology. Someone very special is waiting for you to notice him or her. Don't take any long trips.

LIBRA
You'll have trouble making decisions. Ask your friends for help, but make up your own mind. You'll meet a lot of new people this year and go out a lot. Beware of stranger who loans you money.

SCORPIO
You will have some very difficult decisions to make. Stay calm, and try to control your passionate nature. Always keep your goals in mind. You might be interviewed on TV.

SAGITTARIUS
You could become a hero. A younger person will ask you a question that could change your life. Be careful of accidents to your feet.

CAPRICORN
What seemed lost will be recovered. You may save someone's life. You will receive money in an unusual way. Older woman will play an important role for two months.

AQUARIUS
You'll receive an unusual request from a long-lost relative. Be careful who you trust. Members of the opposite sex will find you attractive. Avoid serious relationships this year.

PISCES
People need your advice. Help them, but save some time for yourself. A computer error could cause you some trouble. Buy some formal clothes – you're going to need them.

When you have finished, look at activity 76.

73

8   You are a tourist staying at the Franklin Hotel. Pick three places on the map below that you would like to visit. Ask your classmate how to get there from your hotel. Make notes as you get the directions, and read them back to your classmate to make sure you understood correctly.

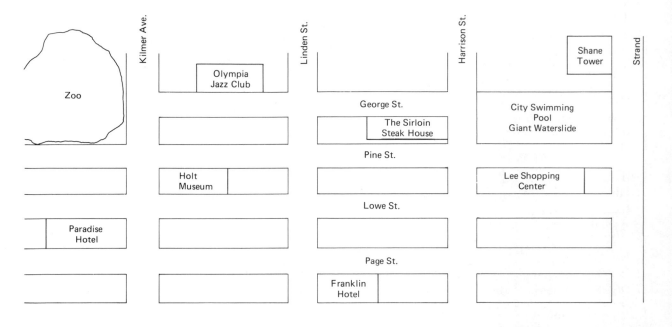

9   You are walking down the street when a radio reporter stops you and asks if you would answer some questions. Agree to do this.

10   The countries shown on page 54 are:
the United Kingdom, Japan, Canada, Australia, Brazil, Chile, France, Greece, Italy, Mexico, Peru, Spain, West Germany, Sweden, Saudi Arabia, the United States, People's Republic of China, Venezuela.

The picture on the right is of JOHN FITZGERALD KENNEDY (1917–1963). He became the 35th President of the United States in 1961, just 14 years after he was elected to the House of Representatives.

In November 1963, he and his wife planned to go to Dallas. His secretary, named Lincoln, advised him not to go, but he went anyway, and was shot in the head on Friday, November 22, 1963, as he drove through Dallas in a Ford Lincoln Continental. He died almost immediately, and Vice-president Lyndon Johnson (1908–1973) became President.

The man who probably shot Kennedy, Lee Harvey Oswald, shot him from a warehouse and escaped to a theater. He died before he came to trial.

Find out what your partner knows about the other picture and discuss the similarities and differences with your own information.

Useful expressions

I think that's . . .
How are they connected? (similar?)
I don't think that's unusual.
There's nothing strange about . . .

That's amazing because . . .
That's really hard to believe.
I can't believe that . . .
What a coincidence!

11

GROUP B   STOREOWNERS

Each of you should pick *one* of the things from the list on page 13. Imagine that you own the kind of store that sells this item. Decide on a realistic price to charge for it. Then find a place in the classroom to open your store, and wait for a customer.

Useful expressions

I'm sorry, but we don't have . . . here.
No. This is a . . . store.
Well, I could give you . . . percent off.
This one is on sale. It's only $ . . .
You won't find a better deal in town!

We have two or three different kinds. This one is $ . . .
You might try . . . I think they have . . .
You're welcome. Come again.

12

OVER 60 POINTS: Others see you as someone they should "handle with care." You are seen as vain, self-centered, and extremely dominant. Others may admire you and wish they could be more like you, but they don't always trust you and hesitate to become too deeply involved with you.

13

14

Ask your partner the following questions and give your opinion too.

1. Do you ever read your horoscope in magazines or newspapers? Is it ever right?
2. Have you ever had your palm read? Did the reader say anything that was true for you?
3. Do you have a lucky or unlucky number?
4. Do you feel like you're a lucky or an unlucky person?
5. Do you wear or carry anything with you to bring you luck or to protect you?

Now answer your partner's questions and listen to his or her opinion too.

15

1. Here are some statistics about the climate in the places on the map. Some of the information is missing. With your partner, try to guess the missing information *before* talking to the others in your group.

	BOGOTA	BUENOS AIRES	ROME	JIDDAH	LOS ANGELES	MEXICO CITY	MOSCOW	OTTAWA	SYDNEY	TOKYO
Warmest month	March	Jan.	Aug.	July	—	May	July	Aug.	Feb.	—
Mean temp. °F.	61	75	77	90	72	—	65	68	72	75
Coolest month	July	July	Jan.	Jan.	Jan.	Dec.	Jan.	Jan.	July	Jan.
Mean temp. °F.	57	—	45	75	57	—	—	10	54	36
Wettest month	Oct.	March	Nov.	Nov.	—	July	July	Oct.	April	Sept.
Rainfall (in.)	55	—	37	8	31	47	28	31	55	—
Driest month	—	June	July	Feb.–Oct.	—	Jan.	Feb.	April	Sept.	Jan.
Rainfall (in.)	24	24	4	0	0	2	4	24	24	24

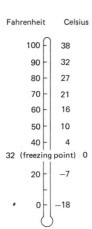

Fahrenheit   Celsius

100	38
90	32
80	27
70	21
60	16
50	10
40	4
32 (freezing point)	0
20	−7
0	−18

2. Ask the others in the group for the missing information. What would you wear in the summer and in the winter in each place? Which places seem to have the most pleasant climate? the most unpleasant?

Your committee is responsible for BUILDING. This includes housing and public buildings like schools, sports centers, museums, hospitals. Work out a plan for the island's future building program. Prepare a brief report to tell the other committees about your plan.

At present there is a primary school in each of the main towns, but there is only one secondary school (in Topa, the capital). Most of the people live in small one-story houses without any modern conveniences. There is one small hospital, one small museum, and no sports facilities.

16

You live next door to your partner in an apartment building. Your partner is having a big party and making a lot of noise. It is after midnight. You have an important business meeting tomorrow and you can't sleep because of the loud music and laughter. You don't want trouble – you just want to get some sleep. Phone your partner and try to get him or her to stop the noise.

17

Useful expressions

Do you think you could . . . ?
I'd really appreciate it if you would . . .
I have to get up early tomorrow.
I don't want to be unreasonable, but . . .

Look, I want you to have a good time, but couldn't you . . . ?
I don't want to, but I could . . .

When you have finished, look at activity 81.

FROM 31 TO 40 POINTS: Other people see you as sensible, cautious, careful, and practical. They see you as clever, gifted, or talented, but modest. Not a person who makes friends too quickly or too easily, but someone who is extremely loyal to the friends you do make and who expects the same loyalty in return. Those who really get to know you realize that it takes a lot to shake your trust in your friends, but, equally, that it takes you a long time to get over it if that trust is shaken.

18

Your partner has a problem. Listen to it and then make some suggestions about how to solve it.

19

Useful expressions

What's wrong?
That's too bad.
Why don't you . . . ?

What you need is . . .
How about . . . ?
Have you tried . . . ?

20

You are walking down the street when a radio reporter stops you and asks if you would answer some questions. Agree to do this.

When you have finished, turn to activity 27.

21

You live in Rockwood. Your classmate will walk up to you on Page Street in front of the Franklin Hotel and ask you how to get somewhere. Look at the map, which includes the bus routes, and tell your classmate the best way to go.

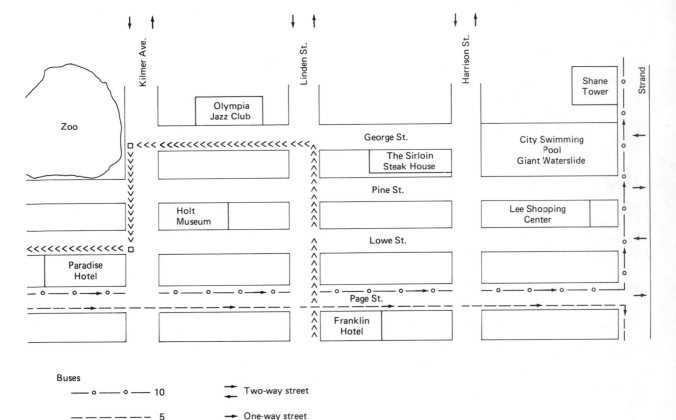

Buses

— o — o — 10

— — — — — 5

>>>>>>>>>>>> 2

→← Two-way street

→ One-way street

Useful expressions

It's a short walk. Go to . . . Street and . . .
*Walk to the corner of . . . and . . . and turn left. Walk . . . block(s) and you'll see
    the bus stop.*
Take bus number . . . on . . . Street (on the corner of . . . and . . . Streets).
Be sure you take the number . . . bus.
Get off at (on the corner of . . .) . . .
You can take either the number . . . bus or the number . . .
No buses go there. You'll have to take a taxi.

You want to take one or more courses at a local college. Call the adult education division and get more information about the courses they offer. Find out

– when the course will begin.
– how long it will last.
– what days and times it is given.
– how much it costs.
– what the official name of the course is.
– as much as possible about what is taught in the course.

22

You might be interested in taking courses in

beginning Arabic	starting a business
art history	motorcycle riding
computers	world religions
photography	dancing

Useful expressions

Do you have/offer a course on . . . ?	*No. I'd like something more advanced.*
I'm interested in . . .	*How often/When does it meet?*
Is it for beginners?	*What's taught in the course?*

When you have finished, turn to activity 68.

A friend of yours has been to two of the resorts, and these are your friend's comments about them. Decide with your partners which of the three places sounds the best and which sounds the worst.

23

	PARADISE ISLAND	PORTO ADRIANO
Scenery	Wild, mountainous, dangerous	Gentle hills with trees and pretty villages in the valleys
Things to do	No nightlife; windy beaches	Visits to old towns, ancient ruins, villages, open-air cafes, and restaurants; swimming
Food	Uninteresting, unimaginative, no good meat	Cheap meals, plenty of variety, delicious fruit
People	Nosy and aggressive	Friendly and hospitable

Useful expressions

I heard that . . .	*I wonder why . . . said that . . .*
I think . . . sounds the best because . . .	*That's funny. I heard that . . .*
But . . . told me that . . .	*I really hate/like . . .*
Well, according to . . .	

24

Read the following ad. Work with a partner and think of good reasons to own this product. Then try to convince the two other people in your group to get it.

When you have finished, turn to activity 56.

25

Answer your partner's questions and listen to his or her opinion too. Then ask your partner the following questions and give your opinion.

1. Do you believe in luck?
2. Have you ever given someone something that would bring that person luck?
3. Do you do anything special before a game or contest to help you win? What?
4. Have you ever made a wish? What do you do when or before you make a wish?
5. When someone sneezes what do you say? Do you know why you say that?

You saw this ad in the local newspaper:

FOR SALE
Used TOYOTA – exc.
condition. $3,000.
Call Pat 938–0472.

26

You need a car, but you can afford to pay only $2,500. Telephone the number given in the ad and find out more about the car:
– How many miles does it have on it?
– Has it ever been in an accident?
– Has it had any major repairs?
– What color is it?

Make an appointment to see and drive the car.

Useful expressions

Hello, can I speak to . . . ?   *I'd like to know (more about) . . .*
I'm interested in . . .   *That price seems a little high.*
I'm calling about . . .   *Do you think I could . . . ?*

When you have finished this conversation, look at activity 86.

27

Now you are the reporter. You work for radio station WRRR, and you have been assigned to stop people on the street and question them for a survey. Introduce yourself and ask your partner these questions.

1. What's your name? Where are you from?
2. Who do you admire the most? Why?
3. What do you do for fun?
4. If you could change places with anyone in the world, who would you become? Why?
5. What is your greatest ambition?

28

You don't feel well. Perhaps you have a headache, a cough, a runny nose, a sore throat, a backache, a stomachache, etc. Tell your partner what's wrong.

Useful expressions

I really don't feel very well.   *I have a terrible . . .*
I feel awful.   *My . . . is killing me.*

When you finish, look at activity 19.

29

Your partner has been assigned to write a short biography of the famous actress Marilyn Monroe. He or she will be asking you some questions. Try to answer them using the information below. If you can't answer a question, say that you don't know the answer.

MARILYN MONROE

American actress — world famous as a sex symbol
Born 1926, died 1962, in Los Angeles, California.
Original name: Norma Jean Mortenson
Had very difficult childhood:
    — mother and grandparents were insane
    — lived in twelve foster homes before she was 16
Marriages:
At 16 married James Dougherty, a worker in an airplane factory. Divorced him after World War II.
Married Joe di Maggio, famous baseball player, January 14, 1954. Divorced him nine months later.
Married Arthur Miller, famous writer, July 1, 1956. Divorced him in 1960.
After World War II she worked as a model. She was discovered when a famous producer saw her picture in a magazine.

Some of her films:
Monkey Business (1952)   *Bus Stop* (1956) — considered one of her best roles
Gentlemen Prefer Blondes (1953)   *Some Like It Hot* (1959)
Seven-Year Itch (1955)   *The Misfits* (1961)

When you have finished, look at activity 46.

30

Imagine that you are a newspaper reporter. Think of a controversial event that has been in the news recently. Interview everyone from the other half of the class to find out how they feel about it.

Here are some possible topics, but use your own topic if you like.

military aid to foreign countries
importance of space exploration
protecting the environment from pollution
bilingual education
mandatory military service

censorship of movies, books, plays
the importance of the Olympic Games
banning cars in crowded cities
apartheid

Useful expressions

Have you heard about . . . ?
What do you think about . . . ?
Do you believe that . . . ?

You work in the adult education division of a college. Someone will phone you to get information about one or more of the following courses. Answer his or her questions.

31

HOW TO START YOUR OWN BUSINESS
Covers market research, financial planning, and legal considerations for starting a new business.
12 sessions   Tues.   6:00–7:45 p.m.   beg. Feb. 5 $250

UNDERSTANDING MODERN ART
Survey of modern art through slide shows and class trips to museums.
12 sessions   Wed.   10:00 a.m.–12:00 noon   beg. Feb. 6 $250

MOTORCYCLE RIDING FOR BEGINNERS
Emphasis on safety, traffic rules, and basic motorcycle maintenance. Must provide your own motorcycle.
4 sessions   Sat.   9:00 a.m.–12:30 p.m.   beg. March 26 $130

COMPUTERS FOR NON-COMPUTER PEOPLE
Make friends with a computer! Learn the basics and see how computers can make your life easier.
4 sessions   Thur.   5:50–8:50 p.m.   beg. Feb. 7 $190

BASIC PHOTOGRAPHY
The secret of taking clear, interesting photographs. Students will develop their own film and make their own prints.
8 sessions   Mon   5:50–7:50 p.m.   beg. Feb. 4 $125, plus $50 lab fee

DISCO DANCING
Join the dance craze and learn to disco!
12 sessions   Fri.   7:45–9:30 p.m.   beg. Feb. 8 $190

When you have finished, turn to activity 40.

Imagine it is Thursday and this is the weather report you saw in the newspaper for Friday and the weekend. Your partner has not seen it. Your partner will telephone you and ask you to do something on a particular day. Decide whether or not you can do it depending on the weather report. If you can't do something one day, discuss whether or not you can do it another day.

32

Friday warm but cloudy and very windy. Possible showers in the evening continuing into Saturday. Thunderstorms developing Saturday afternoon with possible tornadoes. Clearing Sunday, fair and hot. Temperatures: Friday 66–75, Saturday 80–85, Sunday 85–90.

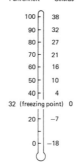

Useful expressions

We can't . . . on Saturday. It's going to rain.

Why don't we . . . on Sunday. It's supposed to be . . .

I'd rather . . . on . . . . I don't like to . . . when it's . . .

That's a good idea. It's supposed to be . . . on . . . .

When you have finished, look at activity 43.

33

You live in Rockwood. Your classmate will walk up to you on Linden Street in front of the Franklin Hotel and ask you how to get somewhere. Look at the map, which includes the bus routes, and tell your classmate the best way to go.

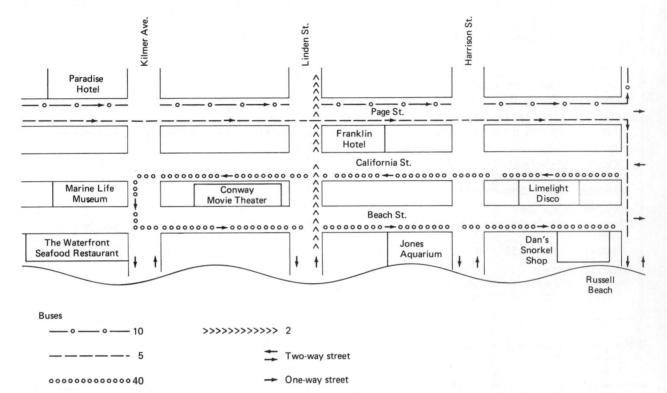

Buses

—o—o— 10

\>\>\>\>\>\>\>\>\>\>\> 2

— — — — 5   ⇄ Two-way street

ooooooooooo 40   → One-way street

Useful expressions

It's a short walk. Go to ... Street and ...
Walk to the corner of ... and ... and turn left. Walk ... block(s) and you'll see the bus stop.
Take bus number ... on ... Street (on the corner of ... and ... Streets).
Be sure you take the number ... bus.
Get off at (on the corner of ...) ...
You can take either the number ... bus or the number ...
No buses go there. You'll have to take a taxi.

When you have finished, turn to activity 8.

34

"Man is born free ..."   *Rousseau*   "All men are created ..."   *Jefferson*
"From each according ..."   *Marx*   "Government ..."   *Lincoln*
"All we are saying ..."   *Lennon*   "In this life ..."   *Franklin*

You are the waiter or waitress in the restaurant. As the people order, write down what they want. Below are lists of the drinks offered at each restaurant. If the information you need isn't given, invent an answer!

35

DRINKS

Soft Drinks
   Coca Cola
   Seven-Up
   Pepsi

Juices
   Orange
   Apple
   Fruit Punch

Beer

The Pizzeria

Soft Drinks
   Pepsi
   Ginger Ale
Beer
Wine

around the world

DRINKS

Iced Tea
American Coffee
Espresso
Cappucino

Turkish Coffee
Beer
Wine

Useful expressions

Are you ready to order?
What kind of dressing do you want on your salad – French, oil and vinegar, or Blue Cheese?

Which vegetables would you like?
Well, we have . . .
I'm sorry. We don't have . . .
What would you like to drink?

36

FROM 21 TO 30 POINTS: Your friends see you as painstaking, perhaps a little too fussy at times. They see you as very, very cautious and extremely careful, a slow and steady plodder. It would really surprise them if you ever did something impulsively or on the spur of the moment. They expect you to examine everything carefully from every side and then, usually, decide against it. They think this reaction on your part is caused partly by your careful nature and partly by laziness.

37

1. Here are some statistics about the climate in the places on the map. Some of the information is missing. With your partner, try to guess the missing information *before* talking to the others in your group.

	BOGOTA	BUENOS AIRES	ROME	JIDDAH	LOS ANGELES	MEXICO CITY	MOSCOW	OTTAWA	SYDNEY	TOKYO
Warmest month	March	Jan.	Aug.	July	Aug.	—	July	Aug.	Feb.	Aug.
Mean temp. °F.	—	75	—	90	72	65	65	68	72	75
Coolest month	July	July	Jan.	Jan.	Jan.	—	Jan.	Jan.	—	Jan.
Mean temp. °F.	—	50	45	—	57	54	14	—	54	36
Wettest month	—	March	Nov.	—	Feb.	July	July	Oct.	April	Sept.
Rainfall (in.)	55	47	—	8	31	47	28	31	—	173
Driest month	July	June	July	Feb.–Oct.	July	—	Feb.	April	Sept.	Jan.
Rainfall (in.)	24	24	—	—	0	2	4	24	24	24

2. Ask the others in the group for the missing information. What would you wear in the summer and in the winter in each place? Which places seem to have the most pleasant climate? the most unpleasant?

38

Your committee is responsible for TRANSPORTATION. Work out a plan for the island's future transportation system. Think about air, rail, road, and sea transport. Prepare a brief report to inform the other committees about your plans.

At present there is a small airport at Topa (it can't take jets), but no deepwater port. There are no railroads and no good roads. Most of the population travels by small boat, bicycle, or on foot.

39

Imagine you are planning to stay home tonight and do something you really like to do. A friend calls you and asks you to go out. Explain as nicely as possible why you'd rather stay home.

Useful expressions

That sounds like fun, but . . .   *I'd like to go, but I can't tonight. I want to . . .*
I really have to . . .   *I'd really like to do that sometime, but tonight . . .*
I wish I could, but . . .   *Thanks anyway for the invitation.*

You want to take one or more courses at a local college. Phone the adult education division and get more information about the courses they offer. Find out:
– when the course will begin.
– how long it will last.
– what days and times it is given.
– how much it costs.
– what the official name of the course is.
– as much as possible about what is taught in the course.

You might be interested in taking courses in

judo	politics
acting	management
math	poetry
speed reading	biology

Useful expressions

Do you have/offer a course on . . . ?   *How often/When does it meet?*
I'm interested in . . .   *What's taught in the course?*
No. I'd like something more advanced.

40

The picture on the right is of ABRAHAM LINCOLN (1809–1865). He became the 16th President of the United States in 1861, just 14 years after he was first elected to the House of Representatives.
On Friday, April 14, 1865, he and his wife planned to go to see a play at Ford's Theater. His secretary, named Kennedy, advised him not to go, but he went anyway and was shot in the head as he watched the play. He died the next day, and Vice-president Andrew Johnson (1808–1875) became President.
The man who shot Lincoln, John Wilkes Booth, shot him in a theater. He escaped to a warehouse, but was shot, or killed himself, before being captured.

41

Find out what your partner knows about the other picture and discuss the similarities and differences with your own information.

Useful expressions

I think that's . . .   *That's amazing because . . .*
How are they connected? (similar?)   *That's really hard to believe.*
I don't think that's unusual.   *I can't believe that . . .*
There's nothing strange about . . .   *What a coincidence!*

42

Talk about spending money with your partner. Answer his or her questions and get his or her opinion too. (If you need some help with ideas, see the list below.) Then ask the following questions.

1. If you had an unlimited supply of money, how would you spend it?
2. If you had less money and had to buy fewer things, what would you stop buying?
3. What things do you hate to shop for?
4. Describe the best-known store in your country or city. What does it sell?
5. What advice would you give a visitor to your country or city about shopping?

Some things you might like to shop for are:
CLOTHES   party clothes, sports clothes, casual clothes
FOOD   gourmet foods, breads, meat
FURNITURE   old furniture (antiques), lawn furniture, camping furniture
BOOKS   mysteries, novels, biographies, science fiction, nonfiction
RECORDS   rock, jazz, classical, folk
ELECTRONIC EQUIPMENT   stereos, computers
TOOLS   power tools, small hand tools
SPORTS EQUIPMENT   soccer equipment, running shoes, golf clubs

43

You want to do something fun this week. Call your partner and suggest some activities for Tuesday, Wednesday, and/or Thursday. Use your own ideas or some of the suggestions below. When you agree on a day and an activity, discuss a time and a meeting place. Write down the information, so you won't forget.

- go to the natural history museum
- go on a picnic
- go for a long walk
- rent some movies and watch them on the videocassette recorder
- go to the park

Useful expressions

Would you like to . . . ?   Let's meet at the . . .
Why don't we . . . on . . . ?   Where shall we meet?
Well, what about Thursday?   What's a good time for you?
Let's . . . on . . .   How about noon?

I told her I had been dreaming about Bubik and it was true: I had awakened from this dream to hear my parents' voices. I knew enough not to tell Basha about the quarrel. I told her I would never see Bubik again, never. It was, to be sure, a thought worthy of tears. Basha sighed. She kept stroking my hair, my wet cheek.

"Well," she said, "maybe some day you'll have another dog."

"No I won't." Mother didn't like dogs, I explained, snivelling; their barking got on her nerves these days.

"Oh well," said Basha. "Don't think about that, sweetheart. Think about something cheerful. Something that makes you happy. That's the secret, you know, that's —"

"What?" I said. "What shall I think about?"

"Oh," said Basha. She considered it for a moment. "Think about the Christmas present I'm about to give you."

I raised my head from her lap, searching Basha's eyes. "A Christmas present?" I said. "But Papa says we don't celebrate Christmas. We aren't Catholics."

"Well, *I* am," said Basha. She would not tell me what the present was, would not give me so much as a clue. "You'll just have to be patient until —"

"When —?" I asked. "Until when, Basha?"

"Only tomorrow," she said. "Only tomorrow, child."

Basha's present was a shiny black music box with a whirling ballerina, a jewellery box, lined in red velvet. I had a turquoise ring and a gold locket, and a chain Mother had given me. Mother was out shopping when I received the present. I told Basha it was lucky the box was meant for *me*.

"Mama doesn't like jewellery boxes," I said, winding mine intently. "She says it just makes things easier for the burglars."

The statement made Basha laugh. She assured me we would find a good hiding place for the box. "I thought you would like the ballerina," she said. "She even looks like you." I had, ever since the age of four when I saw the Bolshoi, been

late on Christmas Eve. There was, in my parents' bedroom, a service bell, built into the wall for summoning the maid. The sound it made was much like that of the entrance bell: a shrill, choked sound, making me jump when rung unexpectedly. It was this bell Mother had arranged to have Basha ring in the early evening. She herself was soaking her swollen feet in the bathroom, calling out to me to get the door.

"Basha's getting dressed," she yelled out. "Go see who it is, Vera."

I opened the door and there was the monkey: a small animal in an enormous metal cage, wrinkling up its face before a tiny mirror. I had, from time to time, been scolded by Mother for fabricating things. I thought: Mother will be angry; she'll scold me when I tell her this. Just then the monkey turned and leapt to the front, blinking at me through the bars. It scratched its armpit vigorously.

"A monkey!" I began to shriek. "A monkey. Basha! Mama!"

My cries were answered by Mother and Basha, as well as our neighbours across the landing. The neighbours were an elderly Jewish couple. The woman sometimes gave me candy, other times failed to recognize me. I had, playing in the courtyard, heard one of the concierge's twins say Mrs. Hertz was crazy. She shrieked in the night, the girl said, right above their bedroom, terrifying them. Mother said she was not crazy; her nerves were bad was all. Basha said Mrs. Hertz was old; she could certainly use a maid. On one occasion, I had seen Basha carry Mrs. Hertz's groceries. Her flat smelled oddly musty, like unwashed socks, but she had excellent candy, wrapped in silver paper. She was speaking to her husband in an odd voice that was not her own; a child's voice, poorly imitated. Her husband spoke to her gently, paternally, shrugging his shoulders at us. After a while, he persuaded her to go back indoors. She gave me a candy just before they left.

"But how would a monkey get here, Mama?" I asked back in our own flat. The monkey sat in its cage on the shiny parquet floor of our large salon.

to midnight Mass. She had [...] leather bag Mother had given [...] was wearing perfume.

"Won't I look grand in church tonight," she said. She smiled at Mother – she had told her a bag was just what she needed – and knelt beside me to look at the monkey. It was a brown, half-grown monkey resembling a bewildered infant. It had small, bright eyes, closely set under a low forehead.

"You mustn't bring your face too close to the cage," said Basha. "It could scratch your eyes or something." The monkey had a swing in its cage: a pine bar suspended from two chains. It kept swinging gently, chewing on its fist.

"Maybe it's hungry," I said, then asked, "What does it eat, Mama?"

"It likes bananas," she said. There *were* no bananas in winter. "And nuts and apples, almost anything."

I asked whether I could feed it.

"Yes – after *you* have eaten." Supper was ready in the kitchen, she said; Father would be late. "Don't say anything about the monkey," she said suddenly. There was in her eyes a bright, mischievous look. "Let him come in and be surprised, all right?"

"Yes!" I loved surprises, though I was often guilty of spilling the beans when I was in on one.

"Don't giggle or make faces," said Basha, mock-frowning down at me. She was going, she said, to wish the concierge's family a merry Christmas but would be back in a little while. At Mother's urging, she ate an open-faced sandwich before going down. Like most Europeans, we ate dinner in the early afternoon; the evening meal usually consisted of cold cuts or wieners with rye bread and mustard, sometimes hard-boiled eggs and herring. Tonight, there was smoked eel, which I had never eaten before. I was eating the eel, asking Mother about monkeys, when we heard the front-door lock turn. Father was home, earlier than expected.

"Remember —" Mother put a finger to her lips. "Not a word about it, eh?"

Father said, "The Finkelsteins didn't make it."

You are the representatives of the Big Burger Company. You want to open a new hamburger restaurant in a certain part of town. You are talking to members of a neighborhood committee. Try to convince them that the hamburger restaurant would be a good idea. Some reasons might be:

1. It will create new jobs.
2. It will make good, fast food available to people in the neighborhood. There is only one other restaurant like it in the area.
3. Big Burgers are delicious and nutritious (good for you).
4. The building is attractive and modern.
5. There will be a playground in the back where kids can play.

Other:

44

Here are six of the languages shown on page 54 with the name of each language and their words for "Thank you."

Danish	Tak
Finnish	Kiitos
Greek	Efharisto
Mandarin Chinese	Xìexie
French	Merci
Polish	Dziękuję

45

You have been assigned to write a short biography (about 10–15 lines) of the famous French statesman Charles de Gaulle. Decide what you want to know and ask your partner questions. Take notes of the answers. Afterward, write your report. You may be asked to present it to the rest of the class.

46

FROM 41 TO 50 POINTS: Others see you as fresh, lively, charming, amusing, and always interesting; someone who is constantly the center of attention, but sufficiently well-balanced not to let it go to your head. They see you also as kind, considerate, and understanding; someone who will cheer them up or help them out.

47

48

1. Talk to another interviewer and decide what questions you should ask the job applicants. Look at (2) below for some ideas and a more complete description of the job.

2. You want to know about the applicant's background – education and work experience. You may want to ask about the applicant's strong points, career goals, and why he or she would be a good manager.

Additional information about the job:

Salary $18,000 a year

Hours 11 p.m.–7 a.m. Thur. through Mon. (Tues. and Wed. are off).

Duties—To supervise 5 night desk clerks and 1 cashier and make up their schedules. Must be able to deal with all problems that the guests or clerks might have. The assistant manager can hope to advance to the position of nighttime manager, then daytime manager, and even manager of all hotel services.

Benefits
Full health insurance, 10 days sick leave a year, and 12 days vacation a year.

The other hotels are in Tokyo, Japan; Mexico City, Mexico; Miami, Florida; Paris, France; Rio de Janeiro, Brazil; Cairo, Egypt.

---

3. Interview an applicant.

Useful expressions

Why do you think you would do this job well?   *Are you sure you could . . . ?*
What experience do you have?   *Have you ever . . . ?*

49

Imagine that you are a newspaper reporter. Think of a controversial event that has been in the news recently. Interview everyone from the other half of the class to find out how they feel about it.

Here are some possible topics, but use your own topic if you like.
nuclear weapons   oil prices or the oil supply
an airline hijacking   government corruption
elections   a sporting event
famine   new laws
capital punishment

Useful expressions

Have you heard about . . . ?
What do you think about . . . ?
Do you believe that . . . ?

When you have finished, turn to activity 67.

You are a travel agent. A customer wants to go to one or more of the following places in June. The customer is going to ask you about the weather there and what kind of clothes to take. Here is some information that will help you. (Use the thermometer below if you want to convert the temperatures to Celsius.)

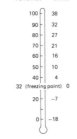

MEXICO CITY, MEXICO   Warm in the middle of the day (70–80 degrees Fahrenheit). Rains very hard every afternoon and is in the 60s Fahrenheit or lower at night.
Light clothes, but include an umbrella, a raincoat, a sweater or light coat, and shoes to wear in the rain.

MADRID, SPAIN   Very hot and dry, with temperatures in the 80s and 90s Fahrenheit.
Light clothes. Shorts should not be worn in the city.

VANCOUVER, CANADA   Usually in the 60s or low 70s Fahrenheit in the daytime and in the 50s at night. Sunny, but good idea to take an umbrella.
Light clothes, but be sure you have several sweaters and at least one warm jacket for evenings.

BUENOS AIRES, ARGENTINA   Cold, with temperatures ranging from the high 20s to the low 40s Fahrenheit. Could be very windy and could snow.
Warm clothes. Include boots and a heavy coat.

Useful expressions

If I were you, I'd take . . .   *You'll probably have temperatures in the . . .*
You'll want to bring along . . .   *It often . . . at this time of year.*
Include . . .   *It could (be) . . .*

When you have finished, look at activity 58.

51

You are at the end of your rope. Your boss has been giving you a hard time all week; you've worked overtime every week for the past month, including weekends. You don't have time to sleep or have fun anymore. You're nervous, tired, irritable – and you have to do something about it. Tell your partner about this problem.

Useful expressions

I can't go on like this any more.   *All I do is . . .*
I wish I could . . .   *I really need to . . .*

52

FROM 51 TO 60 POINTS: Your friends see you as an exciting, highly volatile, rather impulsive personality; a natural leader, quick to make decisions (though not always the right ones). They see you as bold and venturesome, someone who will try anything – well, almost anything – once; someone who takes a chance and enjoys an adventure. They enjoy being in your company because of the excitement you radiate.

53

Imagine that you work in the following movie theaters. When your partner telephones, give the information he or she asks for.

NIGHTMARE ON ELM STREET
Olympia Theater, 2041 Broadway
Shows at 2:50, 5:00, 7:10, 9:20
Admission $4.50

DEATH WISH 3
Bay Cinema, 2nd Avenue at 32nd Street
Shows at 1:45, 3:45, 5:45, 7:45, 9:45
Admission $4.50

THE MALTESE FALCON
Movieland, 36 East 8th Street
Shows at 12:00, 1:50, 3:40, 5:30, 7:20, 9:10
Admission $4.50 evenings and weekends;
   $2.00 weekdays before 5 p.m.

GONE WITH THE WIND
Eastside Cinema, 3rd Avenue
   at 55th Street
Shows at 1:00, 4:00, 7:00
Admission $4.00

Useful expressions

There's a show at . . .   *It gets out at . . .*
Show times are . . .   *We're located at . . .*

When you have finished, turn to activity 87.

54

GROUP A   CUSTOMERS
Each of you should pick *one* thing that you want to buy from the list on page 13. Decide on how much you are willing to pay. Then stand up and go from store to store trying to find what you want at a price you can afford. You might want to shop around and see if you can get it at a cheaper price somewhere else.

Useful expressions

I'm looking for . . .
Can I get . . . here?
Where can I find . . . ?
Do you have any that are less expensive?

Thank you. I'll have to think about it.
Oh, well, thanks anyway.
Thanks. Maybe I'll come back later.
Thank you for your help.

55

You want to go out and do something: go to a movie, go to a football game, go dancing, etc. Call your friend and try to convince him or her to go with you.

Useful expressions

I was wondering if you'd like to . . .
Why don't we . . . ?
How about going . . . ?
I was thinking that it would be fun to . . .

Oh, come on. You can . . . some other time.
Why can't you . . . ?
Well, if you really have to.

Read the following ad. Work with a partner and think of good reasons to use this service. Then try to convince the other two people in your group to use it.

You are going to be interviewed by several newspaper reporters about some current events. Answer their questions.

When you have finished, turn to activity 30.

58

You need to take a business trip in June to one of these places:

Venice, Italy   Nairobi, Kenya
Helsinki, Finland   Manila, Philippines

Go to your travel agent and ask about the weather there and what kind of clothes you should take.

Useful expressions

What will the weather be like in . . . ? *Does it rain that time of year?*
Do you think I'll need . . . ?   *Is it OK to wear . . . ?*
Will it get cold at night?

59

You are a tourist staying at the Franklin Hotel. Pick three places on the map below that you would like to visit. Ask your classmate how to get there from your hotel. Make notes as you get the directions, and read them back to your classmate to make sure you understood correctly.

When you have finished, turn to communication activity 21.

You live in a neighborhood where the Big Burger Company wants to open a new hamburger restaurant. You and your neighbors do not want the restaurant. Talk to the representatives of Big Burger, and tell them why you don't think the restaurant is a good idea. Some reasons might be:

60

1. The building is ugly.
2. The area around the restaurant will be very noisy.
3. Everything at Big Burger is fried and very unhealthy. Fast food isn't good for you.
4. There will be a lot of garbage – this may attract rats and make the neighborhood smell bad.
5. There are enough places to buy lunch already.

Other:

You have just finished eating in a nice, fairly expensive restaurant. There was something wrong with everything you ordered. You could almost never get the waiter's attention, and when you did, he was slow and rude. Explain to the manager of the restaurant why you are unhappy and say what you want to be done about it.

61

Useful expressions

I don't like to be unpleasant, but I really had a terrible meal.
The . . . was too . . . and the . . . was . . .
This was one of the worst meals I've ever had!
I'm not leaving a tip because . . .

UNDER 21 POINTS: People think you are shy, nervous, and indecisive, someone who needs to be looked after, who always wants someone else to make the decisions and who doesn't want to get involved with anyone or anything. They see you as a worrier, who sees problems that don't exist. Some people think you are boring. Only the people who know you well know that you aren't. The trouble is that you don't let very many people get close to you.

62

63

A friend of yours has been to two of the resorts, and these are your friend's comments about them. Decide with your partners which of the three places sounds the best and which sounds the worst.

	PORTO ADRIANO	HIDDEN BEACH
Scenery	Rocky beaches, no sand, terrible for sunbathing	Long, sandy beaches with palm trees
Things to do	Interesting sightseeing (but weather generally too hot), swimming	Sunbathing, waterskiing, tennis, sailing
Food	Cheap but not very good, fruit OK	Lots of good, inexpensive restaurants; lots of different kinds of food
People	Pretend to be friendly to get a tip	Quiet, modest, and shy

Useful expressions

I heard that . . .
I think . . . sounds the best because . . .
But . . . told me that . . .
Well, according to . . .

I wonder why . . . said that . . .
That's funny. I heard that . . .
I really hate/like . . .

64

Your name is Pat and you have a four-year-old Toyota you want to sell for $3,000. It has 70,000 miles on it. It has been a very reliable car – it's never been in an accident, and it always starts, even in cold weather. It has never needed major repairs. It is red and the exterior is in excellent condition. You are selling it because you need a bigger car. You have already seen the new car you want to buy, so you want to sell this one quickly.

Tell the caller that you are willing to discuss the price, and persuade him or her to come over and look at the car.

Useful expressions

This is he/she.
Well, it's/there's . . .
We can discuss the price.
I can't see you tonight, but could you come over . . . ?

It's really been a great car.
I've never had any trouble with it.
Why don't you come over and take a look at it?

When you have finished, turn to activity 72.

Read the following ad. Work with a partner and think of good reasons to use this service. Then try to convince the other two people in your group to use it.

65

LEARN ANY OF 12 LANGUAGES BY PHONE!!

Learn a language in only 15 weeks—and never leave your home or office.
★ Trained teachers, all native speakers, call you at your home or office
★ A new method that is easy, interesting, and gives fast results
★ No memorizing, no stress, no homework
★ Beginner, intermediate and advanced courses tailored to your needs
★ Fluency in 15 weeks guaranteed
★ Special classes for travel, professional and business needs
★ Open 24 hours a day
For a free sample lesson call
PHONESCHOOL
533-0295

You want to do something fun next weekend. Call your partner and suggest some activities for Friday, Saturday, and/or Sunday. Use your own ideas or some of the suggestions below. When you agree on a day and an activity, discuss a time and a meeting place. Write down the information, so you won't forget.

66

- go swimming
- go to the zoo
- play tennis (golf, baseball, etc.)
- go to a movie

Useful expressions

Would you like to . . . ?
Why don't we . . . on . . .
Well, what about Sunday, then?
Let's . . . on . . .

Let's meet at the . . .
Where shall we meet?
What's a good time for you?
How about 1:30?

When you have finished, look at activity 74.

You are going to be interviewed by several newspaper reporters about some current events. Answer their questions.

67

68

You work in the adult education division of a college. Someone will phone you to get information about one or more of the following courses. Answer his or her questions.

JUDO – Beginner's level
An introduction to judo.
12 sessions   Fri. 9:00–10:30 a.m.   beg. Feb. 6 $190

ACTING I
Acting exercises and techniques. No previous acting experience necessary.
10 sessions   Thur. 7:50–10:00 p.m.   beg. Feb. 6 $220

FUN WITH MATHEMATICS
Math can be fun. The perfect mathematics course for people who hate math. Topics include games, algebra, puzzles.
8 sessions   Mon. 6:00–8:00 p.m.   beg. Feb. 2 $160

SPEED READING
Learn to read faster than you ever imagined possible: up to 5,000 words a minute.
12 sessions   Tues. 7:00–9:00 p.m.   beg. Feb. 3 $250

THE POLITICS OF HUNGER
What role does politics play in famine relief? What are the political consequences of hunger? This exploration will focus on current events, especially the famine in Africa.
8 sessions   Mon. 6:30–8:00 p.m.   beg. Feb. 2 $180

DEVELOPING MANAGEMENT SKILLS
How to manage your time and assistants so that your work gets done quickly and efficiently.
10 sessions   Wed. 7:00–9:00 p.m.   beg. Feb. 4 $220

69

Here are six of the languages shown on page 54 with the name of each language and their word for "Thank you."

Swahili	Asante
Spanish	Gracias
German	Danke
Portuguese	Obrigado
Italian	Grazie
Japanese	Dōmo Arigatō

You are a travel agent. A customer wants to go to one of the following places in June. The customer is going to ask you about the weather there and what kind of clothes to take. Here is some information that will help you. (Use the thermometer below if you want to convert the temperatures to Celsius.)

Fahrenheit	Celsius
100	38
90	32
80	27
70	21
60	16
50	10
40	4
32 (freezing point)	0
20	−7
0	−18

VENICE, ITALY   Very hot and humid. Temperatures in the 80s and 90s Fahrenheit during the day and in the 70s at night. Light clothes.

HELSINKI, FINLAND   Warm in the daytime, cool at night. Usually humid, rains almost every day. High 70s Fahrenheit in the daytime; high 60s at night. (At this time of year, the sun sets about 11 p.m. and rises around 2 a.m.)
Light clothes, with a sweater for nights. Include an umbrella and a light raincoat. Also insect repellant if planning to leave the city. Lots of mosquitoes.

NAIROBI, KENYA   June is coolest time of year. In the daytime temperatures are in the 70s Fahrenheit. Cooler in the early mornings and at night.
Light clothes, but include a sweater or light jacket.

MANILA, PHILIPPINES   Hot and humid day and night with temperatures in the high 80s and 90s Fahrenheit. Rain probable – June is beginning of rainy season. Rains could be heavy.
Light clothes. Include an umbrella and a light raincoat.

Useful expressions

If I were you, I'd take . . .
Include . . .
You'll want to bring along . . .
You'll probably have temperatures in the . . .
It often . . . this time of year.
It could (be) . . .

70

You live in an apartment building and you are having a big party. It is after midnight. A neighbor phones to complain that the party is too noisy. You want to stay on good terms with your neighbor, but you don't think you are being too noisy. Talk to your neighbor.

Useful expressions

I'm celebrating because . . .
Why don't you come over and join us?
Look, I know we're playing music, but . . .
I really wish you . . .

When you have finished, look at activity 61.

71

72

You and a friend of yours really want to go to the Michael Jackson concert, but it's sold out. You saw this ad in the newspaper:

> **FOR SALE**
> Four great seats for Michael Jackson concert Mar. 15. All four for $100. Call 223–0659.

There are only two of you and you don't need four seats. Telephone and find out more about the tickets. Try to talk the person into selling you only two tickets and try to arrange a meeting.

Useful expressions

Hello, I'm calling about . . .
I'd like to know (more about) . . .
Do you think I could . . . ?
Would it be possible to . . . ?
Could we meet . . . ?

73

1. Talk to another applicant. Discuss what kinds of questions the interviewer might ask you. How will you answer? Decide what questions you should ask the interviewer. Look at (2) below for some ideas.

2. You want to show the interviewer that you are sure of yourself, friendly, courteous, smart and ambitious. Be sure you have an answer if he or she asks you where you want to be in five years or what your goals for the future are. Also be able to answer the question, "Why do you think you would be good in this job?" Don't ask immediately about salary and raises, but before the interview is over, you should know:
   - what benefits the company offers
   - what the opportunities to advance are
   - what your salary will be.
   You may also want to know what countries the other hotels are in.

3. Talk to an interviewer.

Useful expressions

Could you tell me something about . . . ?
I'd like to know . . .
What are the possibilities of . . . ?
Just one more thing . . .

Imagine it is Monday and this is the weather report you saw in the newspaper for this week. Your partner has not seen it. Your partner will telephone you and ask you to do something on a particular day. Decide whether or not you can do it depending on the weather report. If you can't do something one day, discuss whether or not you can do it another day.

74

Tuesday clear and sunny, cooler than normal. Wednesday clear, hot, and very humid, showers possible in the evening. Thursday light rain in the morning turning into thundershowers in the afternoon. Temperatures: Tuesday 65–72, Wednesday 85–90, Thursday 85–90.

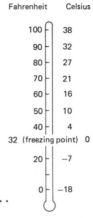

Useful expressions

We can't . . . on Thursday. It's supposed to rain.
Why don't we . . . on Tuesday? It's supposed to be . . .
I'd rather . . . on . . . I don't like to . . . when it's . . .
That's a good idea. It's suppose to be . . . on . . .

Talk about spending money with your partner. Ask him or her the following questions and give your opinion too. (If you need some help with ideas, see the list below.) Then answer his or her questions.

75

1. Do you like to go shopping? Why or why not?
2. What do you like to shop for the best?
3. Would you rather spend money on *things*, or would you rather spend it on entertainment?
4. What kind of stores do you like the most? Why?
5. Describe the best-known store in your country or city. What does it sell?

Some things you might like to shop for are:
CLOTHES   party clothes, sports clothes, casual clothes
FOOD   gourmet food, breads, meat
FURNITURE   old furniture (antiques), lawn furniture, camping furniture
BOOKS   mysteries, novels, biographies, science fiction, nonfiction
RECORDS   rock, jazz, classical, folk
ELECTRONIC EQUIPMENT   stereos, computers
TOOLS   power tools, small hand tools
SPORTS EQUIPMENT   soccer equipment, running shoes, golf clubs

76

Look at the information below and figure out what your astrological sign is. Then ask your partner to tell you about your future. Find the signs for one or two other people who are important in your life. Ask your partner about their future.

Each astrological sign has two dates next to it. If you were born on one of the dates or between the two dates, that is your sign.

Aries	March 21–April 19
Taurus	April 20–May 20
Gemini	May 21–June 20
Cancer	June 21–July 22
Leo	July 23–August 22
Virgo	August 23–September 22
Libra	September 23–October 22
Scorpio	October 23–November 21
Sagittarius	November 22–December 21
Capricorn	December 22–January 19
Aquarius	January 20–February 18
Pisces	February 19–March 20

When you have finished, look at activity 7.

77

Imagine that you work at Ticket Exchange, an agency that sells tickets for different events. Your partner will be phoning you for some ticket information. Give your partner the information. (If you don't know the answer, invent one!)

FLAMENCO FIRE
Carnegie Hall
Sun.–Wed. at 8 p.m.
Tickets $14.50, $12.50, and $10.50
Sold out for Sun., only $10.50 tickets
  available for Wed.

TINA TURNER
Allentown Fairgrounds
Fri. and Sat. at 7:30 p.m.
All tickets $16
Sold out Sat., seats in last 5 rows only on Fri.

SUMO WRESTLING
Madison Square Garden
Every day except Mon. for 2 weeks starting today
Tickets $35, $15, $10
No more $35 tickets left for weekends. Student
  tickets available 1 hour before match begins for $8.

JAZZ FESTIVAL
On Pier 11 at the end of South Street
7:30 p.m. Tues.–Fri., 8:00 p.m. Sat.
Tickets $10. Students $5.

BOSTON SYMPHONY ORCHESTRA
Symphony Hall
Tomorrow only – one performance:
  2:30 matinee
Tickets $20, $16, $12

Useful expressions

The . . . begins at . . .
I'm sorry, but there are no seats available for . . .

How many tickets do you need?
There are only $ . . . tickets left.

Your partner has been assigned to write a short biography of the famous French politician Charles de Gaulle. He or she will be asking you some questions. Try to answer them using the information below. If you can't answer a question, say that you don't know the answer.

CHARLES DE GAULLE

French soldier and statesman
Complete name: Charles-André-Marie-Joseph de Gaulle
Born 1890, died 1970. Born in Lille, in the north of France.
Wrote fiction when he was a teenager, and later wrote several
    nonfiction books.
Married Yvonne Vendroux in 1921. They were married 49
    years.
Served in army 1913–1944. Served with distinction in World War I and led
    the French war effort outside of France (the Free French) in World War II.
Became president of the French Fifth Republic in 1958 and served until 1969.

His achievements include:
– strengthening the role of the presidency
– giving political independence to 12 African territories
– ending the Algerian war (1962)
– restoring France to its former high status in world affairs
– making international policy independent of Communist and Western
    powers

A friend of yours has been to two of the resorts, and these are your friend's comments about them. Decide with your partners which of the three places sounds the best and which sounds the worst.

	PARADISE ISLAND	HIDDEN BEACH
Scenery	Wild, unspoiled, wonderful	Flat, dry, depressing
Things to do	Walking, bird watching, horseback riding	Sunbathing, but often cloudy
Food	Good, fresh seafood	Tasteless, no fresh food
People	Outgoing, talkative, helpful	Don't like foreigners, very unfriendly

Useful expressions

I heard that ...
I think ... sounds the best because ...
But ... told me that ...
Well, according to ...

I wonder why ... said that ...
That's funny. I heard that ...
I really hate/like ...

80

Tell the waiter or waitress what you would like to order. Since the drinks aren't on the menu, you will have to ask what there is to drink. You can also ask the waiter to explain what's in some of the dishes.

Useful expressions

I'd like ...   *Do you have ...?*
What kind of wine/beer do you have?   *I'd like to start with ...*
What would you suggest?   *And then I'll have ...*

81

You are the manager of a nice, fairly expensive restaurant. One of the customers in the restaurant has been complaining all night. This customer has just finished his or her meal and has asked to talk to you.

Useful expressions

How can I help you?   *I'll be happy to ...*
I'm sorry that ..., but ...   *I apologize for ... and I'll ...*
I'm sure the waiter didn't mean to ...

82

These jobs are ranked according to how well-paid they are, on an average, in the United States.

1. doctor
2. lawyer
3. chemical engineer
4. computer systems analyst
5. bus driver (big city)
6. accountant
7. mail carrier
8. police officer
9. flight attendant
10. electrician
11. teacher (primary school)
12. firefighter
13. plumber
14. nurse

(Based on information in the *Occupational Outlook Handbook*, 1984–1985.)

83

Here are some possible stores you could go to:

drugstore   gift shop
shoe repair store   stationery store
hardware store   jewelry store
bookstore   antique shop
candy store   music store
shoe store

Score your own quiz.

Points:

1.	(a) 2	4.	(a) 4	8.	(a) 6	10.	(a) 4
	(b) 4		(b) 6		(b) 7		(b) 2
	(c) 6		(c) 2		(c) 5		(c) 3
2.	(a) 6		(d) 1		(d) 4		(d) 5
	(b) 4	5.	(a) 6		(e) 3		(e) 6
	(c) 7		(b) 4		(f) 2		(f) 1
	(d) 2		(c) 3		(g) 1		
	(e) 1		(d) 5	9.	(a) 7		
3.	(a) 4		(e) 2		(b) 6		
	(b) 2	6.	(a) 6		(c) 4		
	(c) 5		(b) 4		(d) 2		
	(d) 7		(c) 2		(e) 1		
	(e) 6	7.	(a) 6				
			(b) 2				
			(c) 4				

Add the total number of points. If you get get over 60 points, turn to activity 13.
If you get from 51 to 60 points, turn to activity 52.
If you get from 41 to 50 points, see activity 47.
If you get from 31 to 40 points, turn to activity 18.
If you get from 21 to 30 points, see activity 36.
If you have under 21 points, see activity 62.

Your committee is responsible for COMMERCE. This includes the manufacturing industry, banking, and tourism. Work out a plan for the commercial future of the island. Prepare a brief report to tell the other committees about your plan.

At present the main industries are fishing, fish canning, and coconut oil production. The few tourists who visit the island love the calm, quiet life there and the friendliness of the people. There are only a few very small, simple hotels. Although taxes are very low, no international company has invested in Boa Boa.

86

You bought four tickets to a Michael Jackson concert. You found out two days ago that neither you nor your guests can go, so you put an ad in the paper to sell the tickets. You would prefer to sell all four tickets together for $100 rather than split them up. The seats are all together, in the center and close to the front.

Useful expressions

Well, I'd rather sell all four together . . .
I'll be free after . . . o'clock . . .
I don't know . . . I'll have to think about it.

87

Look at the ads on page 34. Pick the sporting or music/dance event(s) that interest you. Then telephone Ticket Exchange, an agency that sells tickets to different events, and get some information about times and prices.

Useful expressions

What time does . . . begin?   *Is there a matinee?*
How much are the tickets?   *Do you have student rates?*
Do you still have seats for . . . ?   *How long will . . . be playing/running?*

88

Here are the complete ads.

HOFSTRA UNIVERSITY
WE TEACH SUCCESS.
50th Anniversary
Hempstead, L.I., New York 11550

WHEN YOU WORK ON A TAN YOU MAY ALSO BE WORKING ON A SKIN CANCER.

THE SKIN CANCER FOUNDATION
Know the signs of skin cancer.

RANK XEROX

The 10 Series copiers. Ready for anything.

Some time ago, Xerox set out to develop a new state of the art. Copiers that would combine the sophistication of the computer age with the durability needed to survive the pace of everyday office life.

We designed copiers that incorporated the very latest technology, and added a few innovations of our own. Then we put them through a course of the toughest tests our engineers could devise.

XEROX 1075 MARATHON   XEROX 1045 MARATHON   XEROX 1035 MARATHON   XEROX 1020 MARATHON

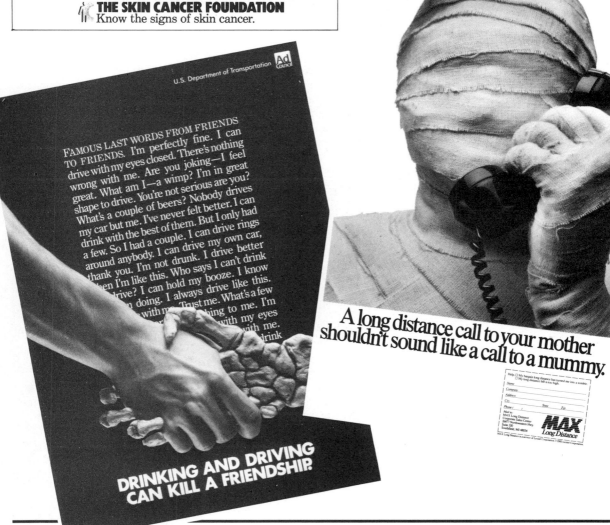

U.S. Department of Transportation

Ad Council

FAMOUS LAST WORDS FROM FRIENDS TO FRIENDS. I'm perfectly fine. I can drive with my eyes closed. There's nothing wrong with me. Are you joking—I feel great. What am I—a wimp? I'm in great shape to drive. You're not serious are you? What's a couple of beers? Nobody drives my car but me. I've never felt better. I can drink with the best of them. But I only had a few. So I had a couple. I can drive rings around anybody. I can drive my own car, thank you. I'm not drunk. I drive better when I'm like this. Who says I can't drink and drive? I can hold my booze. I know what I'm doing. I always drive like this. Stay with me. Trust me. What's a few beers. Nothing's going to happen to me. I'm going to drive with my eyes closed. Stay with me. I can drink...

DRINKING AND DRIVING CAN KILL A FRIENDSHIP.

A long distance call to your mother shouldn't sound like a call to a mummy.

MAX Long Distance

Acknowledgments

Great Ideas is based on the British text *Ideas* by Leo Jones, first published in 1984.

The authors and publisher are grateful to the authors, publishers, and others who have given permission for the use of copyright material: Hold the Mustard Productions for the photographs on pp. 6 and 11; The Bettmann Archive for the photographs on pp. 7 (Lincoln), 29 (top right, middle, bottom left), 87; UPI/Bettmann Newsphotos for the photographs on pp. 8, 51 (top middle), 56 (trophy), 89, 100, 103, 106; Victoria and Albert Museum for details from the Bayeux Tapestry on p. 28; Topham for top-left photograph and BBC Hulton Picture Library for bottom-right photograph on p. 29; Marc P. Anderson for the photographs on pp. 33 (roller skater, flutists), 48 (all except lower left), 56 (demonstration); Fuji-Sankei Communications Group in association with ICM Artists, Ltd. (sumo wrestling), New Line Cinema (*Nightmare on Elm Street*) and Globe Photos, *The Morning Call,* Allentown, PA (Tina Turner), Erwin Frankel Productions Worldwide, Ltd., New York City (Flamenco Fire) for the advertisements on p. 34; Museum of Modern Art Film Stills Archive for the *Maltese Falcon* advertisement (© United Artists Corporation) and photograph of Charles Bronson (© Dino De Laurentis Corp.) on p. 34, scenes from *On Golden Pond* (© Universal City Studios Inc.) on p. 35, scene from *Soylent Green* (© 1973 Metro-Goldwyn Mayer, Inc.) on p. 39, and photograph of Marilyn Monroe on pp. 71 and 82; *TypeWorld* for cartoon by Bob Glueckstein on p. 40; *Time Magazine* for the photograph by Ted Thai on p. 42; American Academy of Pediatrics for the lower-left photograph on p. 48; Japan Air Lines (top left), Greek National Tourist Association (Acropolis), Galloway (pyramid), French Government Tourist Office (Eiffel Tower), India Consulate General (Taj Mahal), and New York Convention and Visitors Bureau (skyline) for photographs on p. 51; 1986 Mexico Tourism for the photograph on p. 53; Reuters/Bettmann Newsphotos for top-left photograph on p. 56 and top-right photograph on p. 65; AP/Wide World Photos for top-right and bottom-left photographs on p. 56; Jeff Cowan, Atlantic City, for photograph on p. 58; Nigel Luckhurst for the photograph on p. 59; *San Francisco Chronicle* for adaptation of article and photograph by Eric Luse on p. 60; American Lung Association for the advertisement on p. 64; Park Advertising/Olympic Airways and Japan Air Lines for the advertisements on p. 67; Hofstra University, Hempstead, N.Y. 11550 for photograph and advertisement on pp. 68, 106; The Skin Cancer Foundation, New York, Fallon McElligott Inc. (for Max Long Distance), and Rank Xerox for advertisements on pp. 69, 107; Calet, Hirsch & Spector, Inc., for the Toshiba advertisement on p. 80; Toyota for photograph on pp. 81, 96; Couples Dating Service, Bethlehem, PA, for advertisement on p. 93.

Illustrations by Elivia Savadier-Sagov: pp. 14, 15, 16, 20, 21, 24, 33, 47, 70 (bottom), 77, 99
Illustration by Mary Jo Quay: p. 12
Illustrations by Chris Evans: pp. 19, 41
Illustration by Dave Parkins: p. 43
Illustrations by David Mostyn: pp. 44, 70 (top)

Book design by Peter Ducker
Cover design by Frederick Charles Ltd.
Cassette production by The Sun Group